The Political Elite and Special Interests

Other Books in the Current Controversies Series

The Border Wall with Mexico
Drones
Fracking
Genetic Engineering
Homelessness and Street Crime
LGBTQ Rights
Political Correctness
Privacy and Security in the Digital Age
Returning Soldiers and PTSD

The Political Elite and Special Interests

Rachel Bozek, Book Editor

GREENHAVEN
PUBLISHING

Published in 2018 by Greenhaven Publishing, LLC
353 3rd Avenue, Suite 255, New York, NY 10010

Articles in Greenhaven Publishing anthologies are often edited for length to meet page
requirements. In addition, original titles of these works are changed to clearly present
the main thesis and to explicitly indicate the author's opinion. Every effort is made to
ensure that Greenhaven Publishing accurately reflects the original intent of the authors.
Every effort has been made to trace the owners of the copyrighted material.

Cover image: Ted Soqui/Corbis via Getty Images

Library of Congress Cataloging-in-Publication Data

Names: Bozek, Rachel, editor.
Title: The political elite and special interests / edited by Rachel Bozek.
Description: New York : Greenhaven Publishing, 2018. | Series: Current
  controversies | Includes bibliographic references and index. | Audience: Grades 9-
  12.
Identifiers: LCCN ISBN 9781534501065 (library bound) | ISBN 9781534501058
  (pbk.)
Subjects: LCSH: Pressure groups--United States. | Elite (Social sciences)--United
  States. | United States--Politics and government--21st century.
Classification: LCC JK1118.P65 2018 | DDC 322.4'30973--dc23

Manufactured in the United States of America

Website: http://greenhavenpublishing.com

Contents

Foreword   **9**

Introduction   **12**

Chapter 1: Are Special Interest Groups Beneficial to Democracy?

Overview: Interest Groups Are Multidimensional   **17**

Green Garage

Interest groups bring several benefits to the advocacy table. However, potential drawbacks—and there are many—can easily detract from this as they come into play within their spheres of influence.

Yes: Special Interest Groups Are Beneficial to Democracy

Strong Backing Often Equals Efficacy   **21**

Michelle Leach

With the right financial and public support, advocacy groups can have a strong influence on outcomes in policy and legislation.

Unions Are Among the Few Groups Representing the   **27**
Middle Class

David Madland and Danielle Corley

While many special interest groups provide upper class Americans with clear representation, unions are among the very few organizations accomplishing this for the middle class.

No: Special Interest Groups Are Not Beneficial to Democracy

Special Interest Groups Do Influence Policy   **32**

Stephane Wolton

How much sway do lobbying groups have? It is difficult to know for sure. Scholars may be failing to capture the full extent of the special interest groups' influence.

Lobbying Has the Potential to Undermine Democratic   **36**
Ideals

George Rennie

As in the United States, lobbying has seen an expansion in activity in Australia. While technically anyone can be a lobbyist, the system favors the powerful, whose money and connections get things done but may not serve the interests of the average citizen.

Chapter 2: Are Widespread Perceptions of the Political Elite Fair?

Overview: The Concept of Elitism Is Nuanced and Complicated   **42**

K. Arjun

There are plenty of grey areas within the concepts defining and surrounding the political elite and elitism. Defining this group and its role is not clear cut.

Yes: Widespread Perceptions of the Political Elite Are Fair

Political Elites Control Power Resources over the Masses   **46**

Luis Garrido Vergara

It is important to understand the importance of social distinction and the theories of power structure when examining the influence of political elites on social change.

Elites Are a Class, Not a Belief   **51**

Natalie Schmidt

There seems to be some confusion about using the term "political elite" as a blanket label for liberals. But that lazy shift in thinking does disservice to the problems with real political elitism.

No: Widespread Perceptions of the Political Elite Are Not Fair

The Caricature of the Liberal Metropolitan Elite Is Inaccurate   **55**

Ryan Shorthouse

Politicians like to use the elite as punching bags for the "ordinary people." But that's just a tactic to pit one group against the other.

"Metropolitan Elite" Is a Lazy Misnomer   **58**

Michael Rundell

The term "metropolitan elite" is unfair and inaccurate. Worse, it's turned into a convenient insult to throw at anyone who doesn't agree with one's views.

Chapter 3: Do Special Interest Groups Keep the Political Elite in Check?

Overview: Interest Groups and Elite Theories Explain **62**
the Driving Forces in Politics

The University of Toledo

Interest group theory is when many different interests compete to control government policy, and their conflicting interests balance each other out to provide good government. Elite theory suggests that a wealthy elite runs the United States.

Yes: The Special Interest Groups Keep the Political Elite in Check

Several Categories of Special Interest Groups **65**
Contribute to the Shape of American Politics

R. Allen Hays

There is a special interest group for almost everyone. No matter how specialized the concern, chances are you can find an organized group with a voice on the political stage.

The Policy Preferences of Special Interests Must **77**
Align with Those of the General Public

James Swift

According to one study, organized interest groups do not correlate with the political stances of the economic elite. But does this mean they serve the average citizen?

No: Special Interest Groups Do Not Keep the Political Elite in Check

The Interests of the Wealthy Dominate the Political **84**
System

Douglas J. Amy

Special interest groups are a primary problem within the US government. They have too much pull over politicians working to do right by the American public.

Money Is the Most Influential Factor in Elections **102**

Rachel Alexander

Corporate contributions in politics are often left-leaning. Citizens United may be one of the best ways for the political right to keep up.

Chapter 4: Do Average Americans Have an Opportunity to Be Heard?

Overview: The Average American vs. the Political Elites   **107**

Martin Maximino

A major study uncovers some alarming truths about the influence of deep-pocketed donors on public policy in the United States.

Yes: Average Americans Have an Opportunity to Be Heard

Efforts to Foster Change, However Small, Can Make a Difference   **111**

Jennifer Earl

When it comes to being heard, any level of activism—including "slacktivism," or "flash activism," can be effective. Voters must become engaged to feel a part of the possibility of change.

Protest Can Rejuvenate Democracy   **115**

Jeremy David Bendik-Keymer

Gathering to protest reminds individual citizens that they have the power to rule a society when they band together to share a cause.

No: Average Americans Don't Have an Opportunity to Be Heard

Corporations Have Tremendous Global Influence   **118**

Ryan Cristián

One striking example of corporate global influence is consideration of the TTIP trade deal by organizations in the United States and EU.

Conservative Lawmakers Strive to Limit Protesters' Rights   **123**

Laura Graham

Protesting is one of the most effective methods for average citizens to be heard. But some lawmakers would like to take that right away.

Organizations to Contact   **126**

Bibliography   **130**

Index   **132**

Foreword

"Controversy" is a word that has an undeniably unpleasant connotation. It carries a definite negative charge. Controversy can spoil family gatherings, spread a chill around classroom and campus discussion, inflame public discourse, open raw civic wounds, and lead to the ouster of public officials. We often feel that controversy is almost akin to bad manners, a rude and shocking eruption of that which must not be spoken or thought of in polite, tightly guarded society. To avoid controversy, to quell controversy, is often seen as a public good, a victory for etiquette, perhaps even a moral or ethical imperative.

Yet the studious, deliberate avoidance of controversy is also a whitewashing, a denial, a death threat to democracy. It is a false sterilizing and sanitizing and superficial ordering of the messy, ragged, chaotic, at times ugly processes by which a healthy democracy identifies and confronts challenges, engages in passionate debate about appropriate approaches and solutions, and arrives at something like a consensus and a broadly accepted and supported way forward. Controversy is the megaphone, the speaker's corner, the public square through which the citizenry finds and uses its voice. Controversy is the life's blood of our democracy and absolutely essential to the vibrant health of our society.

Our present age is certainly no stranger to controversy. We are consumed by fierce debates about technology, privacy, political correctness, poverty, violence, crime and policing, guns, immigration, civil and human rights, terrorism, militarism, environmental protection, and gender and racial equality. Loudly competing voices are raised every day, shouting opposing opinions, putting forth competing agendas, and summoning starkly different visions of a utopian or dystopian future. Often these voices attempt to shout the others down; there is precious little listening and considering among the cacophonous din. Yet listening and considering, too, are essential to the health of a democracy. If controversy is democracy's lusty lifeblood, respectful listening and careful thought are its higher faculties, its brain, its conscience.

Current Controversies does not shy away from or attempt to hush the loudly competing voices. It seeks to provide readers with as wide and representative as possible a range of articulate voices on any given controversy of the day, separates each one out to allow it to be heard clearly and fairly, and encourages careful listening to each of these well-crafted, thoughtfully expressed opinions, supplied by some of today's leading academics, thinkers, analysts, politicians, policy makers, economists, activists, change agents, and advocates. Only after listening to a wide range of opinions on an issue, evaluating the strengths and weaknesses of each argument, assessing how well the facts and available evidence mesh with the stated opinions and conclusions, and thoughtfully and critically examining one's own beliefs and conscience can the reader begin to arrive at his or her own conclusions and articulate his or her own stance on the spotlighted controversy.

This process is facilitated and supported in each Current Controversies volume by an introduction and chapter overviews that provide readers with the essential context they need to begin engaging with the spotlighted controversies, with the debates surrounding them, and with their own perhaps shifting or nascent opinions on them. Chapters are organized around several key questions that are answered with diverse opinions representing all points on the political spectrum. In its content, organization, and methodology, readers are encouraged to determine the authors' point of view and purpose, interrogate and analyze the various arguments and their rhetoric and structure, evaluate the arguments' strengths and weaknesses, test their claims against available facts and evidence, judge the validity of the reasoning, and bring into clearer, sharper focus the reader's own beliefs and conclusions and how they may differ from or align with those in the collection or those of classmates.

Research has shown that reading comprehension skills improve dramatically when students are provided with compelling, intriguing, and relevant "discussable" texts. The subject matter of these collections could not be more compelling, intriguing, or urgently relevant to today's students and the world they are poised to inherit. The anthologized articles also provide the basis for stimulating, lively, and passionate classroom debates. Students who are compelled to anticipate objections to their own argument and identify the flaws in those of an opponent read more carefully, think more critically, and steep themselves in relevant context, facts, and information more thoroughly. In short, using discussable text of the kind provided by every single volume in the Current Controversies series encourages close reading, facilitates reading comprehension, fosters research, strengthens critical thinking, and greatly enlivens and energizes classroom discussion and participation. The entire learning process is deepened, extended, and strengthened.

If we are to foster a knowledgeable, responsible, active, and engaged citizenry, we must provide readers with the intellectual, interpretive, and critical-thinking tools and experience necessary to make sense of the world around them and of the all-important debates and arguments that inform it. We must encourage them not to run away from or attempt to quell controversy but to embrace it in a responsible, conscientious, and thoughtful way, to sharpen and strengthen their own informed opinions by listening to and critically analyzing those of others. This series encourages respectful engagement with and analysis of current controversies and competing opinions and fosters a resulting increase in the strength and rigor of one's own opinions and stances. As such, it helps readers assume their rightful place in the public square and provides them with the skills necessary to uphold their awesome responsibility—guaranteeing the continued and future health of a vital, vibrant, and free democracy.

Introduction

"Who governs? Who really rules? To what extent is the broad body of US citizens sovereign, semi-sovereign, or largely powerless?"

—Martin Gilens and
Benjamin I. Page

Before taking a deep dive to evaluate the relationship—or perceived relationships, depending on where you stand on these issues—between the political elite and special interests, it's critical to look at each of them individually.

"From the eight-hour workday to social safety nets such as Medicare, we owe many of the rights we take for granted to the work of special interest groups."[1]

"Money in politics and corresponding government corruption affect all Americans."[2]

When it comes to special interest groups, the concepts expressed in the above quotations demonstrate the clear division in popular viewpoints. The argument that special interest groups are beneficial to American democracy is hard to dispute, particularly when the fates of often underrepresented individuals or groups hang in the balance. Several of these are explained in viewpoints that follow in this resource.

Alternatively, many believe that special interest groups and their leaders are not ultimately concerned about society at large or the greater good—that they only intend to look out and advocate for those with the same goals as theirs. At this point, it's only fair to wonder: Do special interest groups really represent the American people?

In Chapter 1, Michelle Leach discusses the influence of advocacy groups over policy and legislation, while David Madland and Danielle Corley zero in on unions and what they're doing for the middle class. Stephane Wolton compares pro-change groups to anti-change policy groups, but argues the impossibility of measuring the influence of anti-change forces. George Rennie examines lobbying in Australia, where, as in the United States, the system favors the already powerful.

And then we have the discussion of the elite. Who are the elite? Is this a real group?

> "The Elite always works in the interest of those from whom it derives its power and authority but still it works against democracy because it believes in the rule of the few."[3]

> "[D]on't trust public figures who respond to serious issues by blaming certain social groups, pitting different people against one another, rather than offering practical public policies."[4]

There is a widespread belief that the political elite exists, and that the "members" of this group most certainly have an unfair advantage and drive government-level decisions. Journalists might cover the definition of the term "political elite" and the concerns or perspectives of people who find the existence of such a group to be problematic, versus those who believe the political elite is an inevitable part of how the government operates (but that with proper checks and balances, it is not problematic).

Regardless of where you land in this argument, one discussion that follows this topic rather naturally is that of whether the perceptions of the political elite are, in fact, fair. In Chapter 2, Luis Garrido Vergara explores the elite's power over the masses, while Natalie Schmidt discusses the accuracy of the term "political elite" as she defines just who the term refers to and whether the context and use of the term is valid anymore.

And what's an on-the-fence reader to do when a writer puts himself into one of these categories? This is what Ryan Shorthouse does as he explains his take on the term. The accuracy of the term "metropolitan elite" is further analyzed and discussed in Michael Rundell's article, where he breaks down its use and meaning. So much of this comes down to language: how these terms are used, and more important, how they're perceived.

After reading the first two chapters, you'll likely be able to identify your own stance on the validity or importance of both special interest groups and the political elite. Once you've reached this point, you can ask yourself whether special interest groups serve the purpose, at least in part, of keeping the political elite in check. Those on the "yes" side of this discussion believe special interest groups have a positive influence on society over the reach of the political elite. However, there are many different kinds of interest groups, and far too few advocate for the average citizen.

However, when special interest groups raise impressive sums of money in very short periods, the argument that their influence is both unfair and unreasonable resurfaces. This conversation inevitably opens the door to the topic of the average American. Does the average American even have an opportunity to be heard amid all of this?

In some situations, as we'll see from authors Jennifer Earl and Jeremy David Bendik-Keymer, special interest groups offer the average American an opportunity to be heard and—even better—to participate on whatever level with which they're comfortable. Still, as Ryan Cristián points out, corporate influence remains incredibly strong.

As many individuals and small groups have learned over the course of American history, the final line of defense is sometimes protest. Enter Laura Graham, who will lay out the current climate for protesters and its potential significance.

Public opinion on each of these topics is as varied as the writers' opinions in this book. You might be surprised to learn where you stand after reading the varied perspectives in *Current Controversies: The Political Elite and Special Interests*.

Notes

1. Michelle Leach, "10 Most Powerful Special Interest Groups in America," Listosaur.com, July 2, 2014.

2. Sam Becker, "20 Interest Groups Fueling Government Corruption With Cash," The Cheat Sheet, August 24, 2016.

3. K. Arjun, "Political Elites: Definition, Role and Criticism of Elitism," PreserveArticles.com.

4. Ryan Shorthouse, "Yes, I am part of the liberal metropolitan elite, and I'm bloody proud of it," *Telegraph*, October 11, 2016.

CHAPTER 1

Are Special Interest Groups Beneficial to Democracy?

Overview: Interest Groups Are Multidimensional

Green Garage

Green Garage is an eco-friendly blog.

Also referred to as advocacy groups, lobby groups, pressure groups, campaign groups or special interest groups, there are a lot of questions surrounding interest groups. Generally, they use different forms of advocacy, where they could influence the public opinion or policies and play a significant role in developing both political and social systems. Also, they diverge in influences, motives and sizes, where some of them come with wide-ranging terms in their social purposes, while others usually focus on and always respond to the issues that are experienced by many people.

Because of the helpful benefits that they provide not only to a certain region, but also to the people who are living there, the presence of interest groups is definitely a great idea. Most of the time, these groups are looking for several purposes to perform actions from shared political, commercial, religious and moral positions, using various methodologies in order to make their plans a success, such as having a very successful policy briefing, poll, media campaign, research, lobbying, research and even a publicity stunt. They manage to achieve this with the support of their political influences, powerful businesses and other resources available to them.

While there are real benefits from interest groups, there are also drawbacks that come with them. Let us take a look at their pros and cons to come up with a knowledgeable decision whether they are more useful to society than not.

"12 Foremost Pros and Cons of Interest Groups," by Brandon Gaille, GreenGarageBlog. org. Reprinted by permission.

List of Pros of Interest Groups

1. *They use a democratic process.*
Interest groups contribute a helpful democratic process to protect certain individuals as alternative in daunting the majority. Because of this, many people have the freedom to express and speak their suggestions and opinions.

2. *They check the power of majorities.*
In the US political system, there exist the principles of democracy, which include the majority rule, but there is also the protection of rights of people who do not belong to the majority. Interest groups, such as those based on gender, ethnic and religious identities, can perform important checks on the powers of the majority.

3. *They have the ability to motivate legislators.*
These groups can easily motivate legislators in promulgating their beliefs optimistically.

4. *They allow for better representation of interests.*
Members of interest groups and other social movements believe that they should better advance their causes and interests, whether it is protecting civil rights, voting rights and the environment, by uniting themselves for collective action. By doing so, they demonstrate strength in numbers when it comes to politics.

5. *They provide positive solutions.*
With their skills and knowledge, these groups can easily provide positive solutions to situational problems faced by political departments, such as the Senate.

6. *They serve as an avenue for political involvement.*
Social interest groups, such as women's rights groups like the National Organization for Women (NOW) and civil rights organizations like the National Association for the Advancement of Colored People (NAACP), serve as an avenue for political

involvement and actions for many people. Providing information to their members, these groups are up-to-date with the political issues that might affect them. Moreover, involvement in these groups can result in a more active and informed citizenry, as well as even make people land into successful political careers.

7. They ensure an outspread dispersal of expenses.

These groups and other social movements seek protection and benefits from the government through activities, like marches, petitions and professional lobbying, of which costs are borne by members in question and by society in general. For instance, social interest groups' actions to raise funds for anti-poverty programs can provide increased aid and other benefits to low-income families and individuals on whose behalf the groups speak. Fortunately, the costs of these programs are dispersed across the society, which minimizes the burden borne by any single individual.

List of Cons of Interest Groups

1. They would often seek for the minority of people.

Interest groups lead to pluralism, which critics contend that there is no common good, as there are many conflicting interests in society. What is good for one individual can be bad for other people. Critics also argue that interest groups would interfere with democracy, as they seek out benefits for minorities rather than the greater good of the majority. For example, the National Rifle Association has repeatedly blocked gun-control legislations, despite the fact that most citizens in the US actually want stricter laws on firearms.

2. They only have one track in mind.

As interest groups usually have a single track in mind, they would only think about and look at their personal opinions, and not at those of the majority.

3. They are only effective for themselves.

Another big argument by critics about these groups is that their system can really be effective only for economic interest groups, which normally have greater financial resources at their disposal. It is also believed that these groups would ignore the interests of the poor in favor of the middle and upper-class, who have more money and time to contribute.

4. They would commit serious crimes.

According to past news, there are interest groups that have committed serious crimes, such as corruption, bribery, fraud, etc. There are even those who were involved in some cases and accused of giving threats to domestic social orders and extremists.

5. They lead to "hyperpluralism."

Some scholars argue that these groups have been very successful and use the term "hyperpluralism" in order to describe a political system that caters only to interest groups and not the people. Too many interest groups have led to demosclerosis, which is the inability of the government to accomplish anything substantial. Critics contend that the government cannot make serious changes, even if they are needed, as competing interest groups hinder it from effectively governing the country.

Conclusion

Based on the pros and cons listed above, interest groups can provide a lot of benefits, but they can also come with drawbacks that cause them to experience serious issues, where many people were shocked to be found guilty in crimes they committed. This is a big reason why most people whom they had helped got disappointed with them.

With the information provided by this article, we can reach a well-informed idea of the things interest groups can bring to our society.

Strong Backing Often Equals Efficacy

Michelle Leach

Michelle Leach's work has appeared on TV and radio stations, as well as in public relations departments, newspapers, and magazines. She is a graduate of Northwestern University and Lake Forest College.

From the eight-hour workday to social safety nets such as Medicare, we owe many of the rights we take for granted to the work of special interest groups. Yet many of these organizations have been criticized in recent years for their enormous influence on American politics, whether by endorsing candidates, funding political ads, or in lobbying for legislation favorable to their interests. There are thousands of such advocacy groups today in the U.S. We took a look at a number of factors, including membership numbers, finances and history, to rate the top 10 most influential special interest groups in the U.S.

10. National Association for the Advancement of Colored People

Some believe the organization that helped stop lynching and racial segregation should also become a relic of the past. Pundits point to Barack Obama's presidency as a symbol of the organization achieving its goals. Others acknowledge racial discrimination remains, but that the NAACP must expand its focus to champion a more diverse array of social issues and services. The NAACP makes a point of highlighting much more recent political victories, such as working to abolish the death penalty in Illinois, Connecticut, New Mexico and Maryland; registering almost 375,000 new voters for the 2012 election; and leading the push to outlaw NYPD's notorious "stop-and-frisk" policy.

"10 Most Powerful Special Interest Groups in America," by Michelle Leach, Listosaur.com, July 2, 2014. Reprinted by permission.

9. National Abortion and Reproductive Rights Action League

The Center for Responsive Politics reported this pro-choice group spent $170,000 on lobbying efforts in 2012. But as with every other group on this list, NARAL's reputation and influence in swaying politicians and the public alike far exceed its monetary assets. Whenever a prospective new Supreme Court justice is nominated, for example, the NARAL examines the candidate's past record and statements on abortion and reports them in position papers. In one notable instance, research the NARAL conducted on Robert Bork pointed out contradictions in his record, leading the U.S. Senate to vote against his confirmation to the high court in 1987. It should be mentioned that the country's oldest and largest pro-life group, National Right to Life Committee, spent $2.3 million during the last presidential election. Another $1.5 million came from its Right to Life Victory Fund. One-hundred percent of its donations went to GOP candidates.

8. AFL-CIO

In the face of union membership falling from 35 percent in the 1950s to 11 percent today, the AFL-CIO has grown by 2.5 million members since 2009. The largest organization of its kind in the U.S., it now represents 12.5 million workers across 50-plus unions. Home health care workers, taxi drivers and domestic workers have driven recent growth. The AFL-CIO is also capitalizing on general frustration over stagnant wages, as well as momentum from nontraditional labor groups such as fast-food workers who have organized strikes. At the organization's 2013 convention, leaders vowed to bolster member numbers and the group's influence by partnering with other progressive groups, including the NAACP and Sierra Club. Some labor movement experts contend this combination of strong membership and alliances could turn the tide for the organization responsible for championing laws to mandate the 8-hour workday and safer working conditions.

7. American Israel Public Affairs Committee

Fortune Magazine once labeled the AIPAC the second most powerful lobby in America. According to AIPAC's website, the 100,000-member group has championed the passage of more than a dozen bills to impose tougher sanctions on Iran and bolster security assistance to Israel in the past 15 years. Israel has been by far the largest recipient of U.S. foreign aid since World War II, to the tune of almost $3 billion per year over the past quarter-century. AIPAC certainly deserves some of the credit for that continuing cash flow. While AIPAC doesn't officially make contributions to candidates, it does coordinate a political financing network of sorts, mobilizing wealthy Jewish-American donors on both sides of the political aisle — including tycoons Sheldon Adelson and George Soros.

6. MoveOn.org

From its early days as an email group, this organization has used online tools to drive petitions on many liberal/progressive issues, from raising the minimum wage to protecting whales. It now counts more than 5 million members, many of whom were involved with Occupy Wall Street. What MoveOn.org lacks in donation size (individual donations in 2014 averaged $20), it makes up for in donor volume, boasting more than 300,000 different monetary supporters since 2010. The group claims several major achievements in recent years, including its work to end the Iraq war, pass health care reform, and elect and reelect President Barack Obama.

5. Americans For Prosperity

While the Koch brothers have been linked to conservative organizations from the Heritage Foundation to FreedomWorks, arguably their best-known effort is Americans for Prosperity. The Washington Post recently called Americans for Prosperity, "America's Third-Biggest Political Party." With a multistate reach, it staffs up for elections and conducts local endorsements for campaigns much like a political party. The Post also claims AFP's planned spending on the 2014 electoral push heading into 2016 would reach an estimated $100 million, with messages specially tailored to reach veterans, Latinos and youths. Thus far, Americans for Prosperity has more than doubled staffing levels to 240 full-time employees, comparable to levels for the entire Republican Party.

4. AARP

The AARP, which began as the American Association of Retired Persons, claims 37 million members and represents the interests of Americans aged 50-plus. When the AARP expresses interest in an issue, politicians, the media and the public take note. Look no further than the AARP's endorsement of the Affordable Care Act (aka health care reform). In addition to offering its endorsement of the law, the AARP championed provisions such as annual wellness and preventive screenings and measures to close the infamous Medicare Part D donut hole. Of course, the AARP also has additional influence through its role selling millions of supplemental health insurance policies to seniors.

While The Association of Mature American Citizens and other groups have emerged as "conservative" alternatives, the AARP contends it supports private options (a bone of contention among right-wingers) as long as Medicare remains a viable option. With 10,000 boomers turning 65 every day, the AARP shows no signs of becoming a fossil as more seniors of all backgrounds and political leanings are staying active and living longer.

3. American Medical Association

A frequent supporter of Republican candidates, the AMA spent around $306 million in lobbying from 1998 to 2014, second only to the U.S. Chamber of Commerce. In 2013, it ranked eighth out of more than 4,100 organizations surveyed in terms of lobbying, spending $18.25 million. Again, money isn't everything in the world of politics. When the AMA announced its support of the Affordable Care Act legislation in 2010, health-care supporters widely trumpeted the news; when a group with more than 200,000 members in a highly respected occupation — physician — supports your cause, that type of influence is almost priceless. Not surprisingly, Medicare and Medicaid represent the top issues lobbied by the AMA in 2013.

2. U.S. Chamber of Commerce

The U.S. Chamber of Commerce is the biggest organizational spender in American politics, according to the Center for Responsive Politics OpenSecrets.org site. Between 1998 and 2014, this organization representing more than 3 million members spent a whopping $1 billion — equivalent to the GDP of countries like Mongolia and Belize. This figure dwarfs the second-biggest spender on the list, the American Medical Association, at a comparatively paltry $306 million. Not surprisingly, the Chamber has overwhelmingly supported GOP candidates — so much so that donations to the group have been deemed "controversial" for some companies with a broad, global customer base; in 2009, for instance, Apple and Nike were among the corporations that "quit" the member-organization, due to its opposition of policies to proactively address climate change.

1. National Rifle Association

An active membership and hefty bank account make the NRA the envy of other special interest groups. The NRA claims 5 million members, and according to BusinessInsider.com, in 2010 it boasted revenues of almost $228 million and assets of $163 million. The NRA's membership and financial health give it enormous clout both in influencing the public and politicians. Think back to the aftermath of the school shooting in Newtown, Connecticut, in 2012. While polls showed public support for more restrictive gun-control legislation, and President Barack Obama pushed extensively for changes, the NRA's lobbying—and the omnipresent threat it posed to Democrats in conservative districts and states—defeated the effort to impose new gun controls. In fact, the NRA cited recent federal efforts to enact new gun-control measures with bringing in hundreds of thousands of new members.

Unions Are Among the Few Groups Representing the Middle Class

David Madland and Danielle Corley

David Madland is the director of the American Worker Project at the Center for American Progress Action Fund. Danielle Corley is a special assistant for the Economic Policy team.

Buried deep inside Princeton University political scientist Martin Gilens's research highlighting the excessive influence the rich have on modern U.S. politics, there is a hidden gem exploring which interest groups best represent the priorities of the middle class. Gilens found that, while most powerful interest groups advocate for policies that predominately benefit their narrowly defined members, relatively few focus on policies that the middle class supports. According to Gilens, most of these middle-class oriented groups are unions, which is a big problem for the United States, as unions have been declining in membership and losing power for decades.

Gilens determined how closely the positions taken by leading interest groups matched up with the preferences of the middle class by measuring the correlations between the policy preferences of Americans at the 10th, 50th, and 90th income percentiles—as recorded in more than 1,000 poll questions—and the public stances of powerful interest groups on these particular questions. Groups were selected from *Fortune* magazine's "Power 25," lists of the most powerful interest groups in Washington during the Clinton and George W. Bush administrations, in addition to the 10 industries with the highest lobbying expenditures. The chart below illustrates Gilens's key findings. The groups listed at the top tend to share the policy preferences of Americans earning near

"Unions Are Among the Very Few Interest Groups that Represent the Middle Class," by David Madland and Danielle Corley, Center for American Progress Action Fund, November 14, 2014. Reprinted by permission.

the 50th percentile, which we define as the middle class, while the groups at the bottom consistently take positions that conflict with the preferences of the middle class. Our figure only includes interest groups where the correlations with middle-class positions were highly statistically significant, but it is worth noting that most of the groups not shown also tended to take positions opposed by the middle class.

Interest Groups Whose Positions Reflect Middle Class Interests

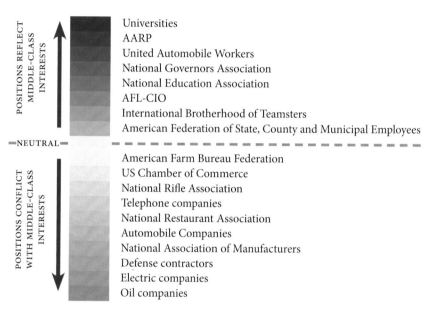

POSITIONS REFLECT MIDDLE-CLASS INTERESTS

Universities
AARP
United Automobile Workers
National Governors Association
National Education Association
AFL-CIO
International Brotherhood of Teamsters
American Federation of State, County and Municipal Employees

=NEUTRAL=

POSITIONS CONFLICT WITH MIDDLE-CLASS INTERESTS

American Farm Bureau Federation
US Chamber of Commerce
National Rifle Association
Telephone companies
National Restaurant Association
Automobile Companies
National Association of Manufacturers
Defense contractors
Electric companies
Oil companies

SOURCE: Martin Gilens

What is striking about Gilens's findings is that all five of the unions studied—the AFL-CIO, the American Federation of State, County, and Municipal Employees, the International Brotherhood of Teamsters, the United Automobile Workers, and the National Education Association, or NEA—and a few other groups, such as AARP, the National Governors Association, or NGA, and the collective advocacy efforts of universities, are among the only groups that more often than not lobby for policies the middle class supports. Many leading interest groups, such as the U.S. Chamber of Commerce, oil companies, and other business organizations, actively advocate against policies that the typical American favors. All in all, of the 40 groups Gilens presented analysis for, only 8 strongly supported the interests of the middle class.

Similarly, the policy positions of these interest groups tend to align with the preferences of the poor, defined as Americans at the 10th income percentile. AARP, universities, the NGA, and unions advocate for policies the poor support, while most prominent interest groups—typically organizations representing business owners—work against the preferences of the poor. Interestingly, most unions, AARP, universities, and the NGA also tend to support policy measures favored by people with incomes at the 90th percentile, though the correlations are not as strong as those with the middle class and the poor and are sometimes statistically insignificant. This suggests that unions, AARP, universities, and the NGA tend to support policy measures that most Americans want, while most interest groups—especially those representing business owners—tend to represent the views of a very narrow constituency.

The efforts of unions and other groups that represent the interests of the middle class and the poor are critical for making democracy work. Few individuals have the time or resources for sustained engagement with the political system, especially among the poor and middle class. Interest groups provide the structure for individuals to pool their resources on behalf of their preferred policies, provide legal and regulatory expertise, and ensure effective implementation of policies—working not only to help pass legislation but also lobbying for implementation once policies have been passed. They also can mobilize members, and often the general public, at key points throughout the legislative process.

Democracy suffers when the most influential interest groups only represent the views of a narrow group of citizens, such as business owners or other rich and powerful people, while overlooking the preferences of the larger middle class. In order for democracy to work for the middle class, interest groups representing the wealthy need to be offset by a counterbalancing force. Indeed, President James Madison, a chief framer of the U.S. Constitution, recognized that interest groups representing all perspectives—not just those of the rich—were necessary for our system of government to function properly. In President Madison's essay "Federalist No. 10," he cautioned that "the most common and durable source of factions has been the various and unequal distribution of property." President Madison's solution to the problem of factions was to ensure that all interests were able to participate in the democratic process in order to provide a check on the other, writing that with "a greater variety of parties and interests; you make it less probable that a majority of the whole will have a common motive to invade the rights of other citizens." But when one interest or faction isn't represented, or is only weakly represented, the checks and balances of the system fail and some interests dominate at the expense of others.

Of the organizations that represent middle-class interests, unions are arguably the most important. While universities and the NGA often advocate for policies aligned with middle-class interests, they generally take positions on a relatively small amount of the policy areas Gilens reviewed. Unions, on the other hand, engage in a large number of issue areas that benefit the middle class, supporting policies such as raising the minimum wage, increasing health care coverage, and promoting retirement security. AARP is another important group, especially when it comes to giving a voice to the needs of older Americans. Unions, however, represent broad swaths of industries and workers and warrant particular attention, as they comprised five of the eight groups Gilens identified with positions that most reflect middle-class interests.

Given that unions have lost power in recent decades—in part because conservatives have been waging a war against them—it is unsurprising that the middle class has not fared well over this period of time. Indeed, the weakening of labor unions strongly correlates with the shrinking of the middle class: As union membership declined, the share of national income for the middle 60 percent of households has fallen to record lows. Harvard University Professor Bruce Western and University of Washington Professor Jake Rosenfeld found that union decline explains one-fifth to one-third of the growth in inequality in the United States over recent decades.

With the increasing influence of interest groups, especially those that represent the narrow interests of the wealthy, the counterweight unions provide in advocating for middle-class interests is even more crucial. If the middle class is to regain its policymaking voice and economic strength, reinvigorated unions will be critical in the fight for their interests. Any agenda to rebuild the middle class needs to include a plan to strengthen unions and empower the workers they represent.

Special Interest Groups Do Influence Policy

Stephane Wolton

Stephane Wolton is an assistant professor of political science at the London School of Economics's Department of Government.

The Influence of Special Interest Groups (SIGs)

The influence of Special Interest Groups (SIGs) is widely seen as pervasive in the United States. Their far-reaching power, as reported in the Press, ranges from the writing of bills, such as arrangement of banks regulations (even after the 2008 banking crisis), to the pressure exercised on more directly perceivable matters, such as delays in the introduction of life-saving measures in railways and public transportations. The academic literature, however, paints a more nuanced picture: It is well documented that legislators voting for (against) a bill receive contributions from groups supporting (opposing) the policy change, but these monetary transfers seem to have little effect on Members of Congress' voting decision. This perhaps counter-intuitive result can be explained by a simple observation: SIGs donate to elected politicians who share their policy preferences but refrain from sponsoring swing legislators. [1]

Scholars, nonetheless, have found that monetary transfers to representatives and/or "informative lobbying" (namely, the transmission of information rather than money, to Member of Congress) have some impact on a number of policies in domains as varied as trade tariffs, firm subsidies or taxes, federal research funds to universities, or the passing of energy bills. [2] How can we explain these apparently contradictory arguments? Is public perception wrong and the influence of SIGs rather limited, or are scholars failing to capture the full extent of SIGs influence?

Theoretical Framework

Most empirical scholarly works have in common their focus on contributions and informative lobbying, referred to as inside lobbying. However, inside lobbying constitutes only one out of the many channels lobby groups employ to affect policy decisions. SIGs can also engage in outside lobbying, that is, activities meant to mobilize the public on some issues (such as those canalized by grass roots movements, political advertising, or even protests). [3] My paper develops a game-theoretic model in which Special Interest Groups can affect the *content* of a bill with inside lobbying and the *fate* of a legislative proposal with outside lobbying. I show that researchers which exclusively focus on inside lobbying expenditures are likely to underestimate both the extent and strength of SIGs influence.

My theoretical framework models the interactions between a decision-maker and two interest groups: a pro-change lobby that shares the policy preferences of the decision-maker and an anti-change interest group that holds opposite preferences. For both types of SIGs, the policy choice of the decision-maker depends on her assessment of how willing the respective pressure groups are to engage in outside lobbying. Mobilization of the public serves different purposes depending on the group engaging in it. The pro-change interest group promises its support and help in the passing of a broad reform, whereas the anti-change interest group threatens to mobilize the public against the proposed change. Importantly, inside lobbying expenditures, in this framework, do not always mirror the outside lobbying capabilities of special interest groups.

Pro-Change Interest Groups

When its resources are high, a pro-change interest group prefers to preserve its war chest for the upcoming defense of the decision-maker's proposal. This implies, in turn, that a pro-change SIG engages in inside lobbying only if it has little willingness to embark in outside lobbying. Inside lobbying expenditures serve the purpose of credibly pleading poverty and thus pressuring the decision-maker into compromising on her proposed reform. In short, because inside lobbying induces compromise, it is negatively correlated with influence. Empirical researchers can, however, recover unbiased estimates of pro-change SIGs influence by considering outside lobbying expenditures. Pro-change interest groups sway policy choices thanks to their promise to engage in outside lobbying, and promises are effective only if acted out.

Anti-Change Interest Groups

For anti-change interest groups, I show that often enough, the mere threat of outside lobbying is sufficient to induce the decision-maker to compromise on her would-be reform. As such, even in the absence of inside lobbying expenditures, anti-change interest groups can have significant influence on policy choices. The empirical focus on inside lobbying expenditures thus severely underestimate the power of SIGs. Unlike promises, however, threats are effective when they are not carried out. Consequently, threats are observed only when the anti-change interest group fails to affect policy choices. Using outside lobbying expenditures, empirical researchers can thus only assess when special interest groups influence decision-makers' proposals, but not how and to which extent they are able to do so. My work, thus, does not only spots caveats in the empirical literature on lobbying, but it also highlights that there exist limits to our ability to understand the power of groups that oppose policy changes.

Summary

To summarise, my paper offers mixed messages for scholars or journalists interested in measuring SIGs influence. First, it clearly indicates that the empirical literature needs to look beyond inside lobbying expenditures. Second, it provides hope for an unbiased estimate of the power of groups favoring policy changes. Lastly, it suggests that researchers may be unable to correctly measure the influence of groups opposed to changes. This last conclusion is not without important implications. Groups blocking reforms have a great sway on the policy process in the United States, and failing to properly assess their power makes it difficult to design adequate policies to curtain their influence.

Notes

1. For a review, see Ansolabehere et al. (2003).
2. See Goldberg and Maggi (1999), Bombardini and Trebbi (2011), de Figueiredo and Richter (2014), Kang (2015).
3. There are exceptions. For example, Bombardini and Trebbi (2011) propose a model in which firms can either contribute to a policy-maker or guarantee the vote of their employees. Other important works are cited in the author's paper.

References

Ansolabehere, Stephen, John M. de Figueiredo, and James M. Snyder Jr. 2003. "Why Is There So Little Money in U.S. Politics?" Journal of Economics Perspective, 17(1): 105-130.

Bombardini, Mathilde and Francesco Trebbi. 2011. "Votes or Money? Theory and Evidence from the U.S. Congress." Journal of Public Economics, 95: 587-611.

De Figueiredo, John M. and Brian K. Richter. 2014. "Advancing the Empirical Research on Lobbying." Annual Review of Political Science, 17: 163-185.

Goldberg, Pinelopi Koujianou and Giovanni Maggi. 1999. "Protection for Sale: An Empirical Investigation." American Economic Review 89(5): 1135-1155.

Kang, Kalam. 2015. "Policy Influence and Private Returns from Lobbying in the Energy Sector." Review of Economic Studies, forthcoming.

Lobbying Has the Potential to Undermine Democratic Ideals

George Rennie

George Rennie is a lecturer in politics at the University of Melbourne, Australia. His research focuses on US politics and lobbying.

Over the past 20 years, lobbying activities in Australia have expanded dramatically. Following the United States' lead, where a radical shift in ideology in the 1970s led to a re-evaluation of the way corporations view their role in society, the notion of corporate "civic duty" has been replaced by a belief that governments and the public are fair game for special interests.

Now, lobbying in Australia is a multi-billion dollar industry which employs a sophisticated strategy to win public opinion and political favours for its clients or members.

Lobbying and the "Revolving Door"

Who is able to lobby, and the methods they can employ in doing so, is determined by a patchwork of laws designed to add some transparency to an otherwise murky process. There are, therefore, "official lobbyists"—individuals and firms for whom the frequency and import of their work requires them to register themselves.

Any interested party can engage the services of these professionals for a fee, but if a board member, union official, or other "concerned citizen" wants to meet with a political decision-maker, and perhaps even discuss a policy or infrastructure proposal over lunch, there's little—other than a vigilant press, perhaps—to effectively prevent them from doing so.

So, political lobbying is not limited to those officially sanctioned as "registered lobbyists". Its scope includes anyone who wants

"Lobbying 101: How Interest Groups Influence Politicians and the Public to Get What They Want," by George Rennie, The Conversation, June 8, 2016. https://theconversation.com/lobbying-101-how-interest-groups-influence-politicians-and-the-public-to-get-what-they-want-60569 Licensed under CC BY 4.0 International.

something and is willing to twist a government official's arm to get it.

Lobbying consists of a range of strategies designed to co-opt or realign policy. Broadly, these strategies attempt to influence one of two key targets: government (including regulators) and the public.

In order to lobby politicians and regulators, lobbyists use campaign donations, letter writing campaigns, and try to build personal relationships. Lobbyists can also rely on morally dubious quid-pro-quo arrangements, such as jobs for friendly politicians at retirement.

This can lead to potential conflicts of interest. In the US, around 50% of ex-legislators become lobbyists. Although not to the same extent, this also occurs in Australia.

Alternatively, lobbying the public relies on advertisements, op-ed pieces, commissioned research, protests, and press releases to try and shift public opinion on a given issue.

Whether politicians or the public are targeted depends on their amenability. When dealing with Labor, for example, the Australian Council of Trade Unions will focus its efforts on meeting privately with Labor, and attacking the Liberal Party publicly. Demonstrations and ad campaigns are used to try and influence public opinion to that end, and played a key role in the 2007 election in attacking WorkChoices.

Similarly, business—which is more likely to have a combative relationship with Labor—will engage with the Liberal and (to a lesser extent) Nationals parties more positively, and engage in "public information" campaigns to exert political pressure on Labor, such as the mining tax campaign in 2010.

But these relationships make it harder for Labor to create policy at odds with union interests; and it's similarly difficult for the Liberal Party to put "big business" off-side. Doing so for either party alienates key allies, and the question of whether a policy is actually "good" for the country can become a secondary consideration.

The Many Faces of Lobbying

While lobbying in Australia represents a wide range of interest groups, it has a high cost associated. This can mean that, to the extent that lobbying is effective, it disproportionately benefits big businesses and a wealthy elite who can afford to "pay the piper".

And if an issue isn't adopted by unions—many important debates aren't— then the associated public debate can be one-sided.

Businesses are generally well represented. Peak bodies, such as the Business Council of Australia and the Property Council, ensure that even small and mid-sized businesses have a say. Further, the largest think-tanks, such as the Institute of Public Affairs, ensure that the ideology of business—low taxes and few regulations—is well reflected in public discourse.

By stark contrast, "grassroots" organisations such as GetUp! or the Australian Conservation Foundation, even when broadly representative of the views of a large proportion of the population, tend to have far fewer resources at their disposal for public relations or campaign financing. To that end, their ability to effectively lobby is severely undermined.

The problem is one of diffusion. Compare, for example, a lobby group that represents very few very-high-income members (be they individuals or businesses) with one that represents many of average or low incomes. If a lobby group thinks a policy might threaten its members' livelihood, it is far easier to draw large sums of money from wealthy few because, proportionately, the risk-reward ratio is much more in their favour.

When a policy is at odds with well-resourced interests, chipping in a few million towards a campaign is far easier to do, as many mining magnates did in 2010.

During that same time, despite claiming a million members, GetUp! was relatively under-resourced financially, and dramatically outspent by organisations such as the Minerals Council. As such, organisations like GetUp! are often forced to resort to social media, and hope that, predicated on humour, outrage or luck, their videos will go "viral".

Election 2016

Elections unfailingly draw the attention and best efforts of lobby groups, which have a lot to gain or lose depending on which party takes power.

Labor has the unions on-side, which have been strangely quiet in the wake of the royal commission. But big business is disproportionately in the Coalition's camp.

The Property Council, along with the state and federal Real Estate Institutes, clearly view the mooted changes to negative gearing laws as a threat. To that end, they're pushing the message that removing negative gearing will devastate housing, one of Australia's biggest industries.

But the dark horse in this race is the banking industry. When Opposition Leader Bill Shorten signalled a royal commission into banks, the immediate response by the industry was to threaten a "mining tax-style campaign".

Labor is still licking its wounds from the 2010 mining industry assault and is keen to avoid a repeat from a similarly well-resourced foe. But it knows the banking industry would be risking a lot in the battle for public sentiment, should it decide to wage a public relations war on Labor.

The Proper Role of Lobbyists

Lobbying plays a critical role in Australia's representative democracy. The sheer plurality of voices in a country of 23 million ensures that Australia needs a system to filter and convey the views of the many to the few who represent them. To that end, the role of the lobbyist is critical.

However, the dangers of lobbying are great. The potential for regulatory and government capture by special interests, as well as the ability of powerful concentrated interests to drown out other voices in public debate, presents significant challenges for Australian democracy.

Consequentially, Australia would benefit from changing to disclosure rules on campaign financing. We should also re-evaluate the permissibility of the "revolving door" of politicians and the lobbying industry. More pressingly, in the wake of recent scandals around political donations, Australia may need a national corruption watchdog along the lines of NSW's Independent Commission Against Corruption.

Not all of these challenges can or should be tackled legislatively, but the potential of lobbying to undermine democratic ideals means reform is needed. The sooner the better.

CHAPTER 2

Are Widespread Perceptions of the Political Elite Fair?

Overview: The Concept of Elitism Is Nuanced and Complicated

K. Arjun

K. Arjun writes about political elitism.

Definition

Aristotle held that some persons are fit to rule while others are fit to be ruled over. Elite means "chosen few." Elite consists of those persons who come at the top because of their superior quality. Such chosen few generally exist in trade-Unions, bureaucracy, armed forces and almost everywhere.

The Elite Theory

The Elite Theory consists of the idea that there are two groups:

(1) The selected few who govern the society because of their ability and

(2) The vast masses who are governed because they are destined to be ruled.

Elite theory assures that men may be equal in the eyes of God but they are not so in the eyes of man.

According to the theorists, inequality is largely found in every state and society, thus making every one of them oligarchical in different degrees. Elites arise in every type of society and state because of the ancient traditions, wealth, physical might, economic status and ability.

"Political Elites: Definition, Role and Criticism of Elitism," by K. Arjun, PreserveArticles. com. http://www.preservearticles.com/2014081433553/political-elites-definition-role-and-criticism-of-elitism.html. Licensed under CC 3.0 BY SA.

Rule of Elite Differentiated from Aristocracy and Oligarchy

"An elite," according to Verney, "appears to combine some of the characteristics of both an Oligarchy (government by the few privileged) and an aristocracy (government by the best) but is not to be confused with either. It is a minority, like an aristocracy but there is neither in the sense of self-preparation and selfishness which often is associated with the latter."

In simpler words oligarchy and aristocracy are both distinct from the elite. Oligarchy is a government by the few privileged and the Aristocracy is a government by the few best but with the Elite there is no grandeur of aristocracy and no desire for self-perpetuation and selfishness as we found in Oligarchy.

The Elite always works in the interest of those from whom it derives its power and authority but still it works against democracy because it believes in the rule of the few. Therefore Maurice Duverger holds the opinion that "government of the people and by the people must be replaced by another formula Government of people by an elite sprung from the people." Consequently, the theory of political elite stands on the principle of natural inequality and is opposed to the liberal democratic state.

Role of the Elite

The role of the elite in the society is extremely important because it formulates the policies and takes the decisions. The elite give political education to the masses and they set certain model standards in the society. It is throughout the elites, writes Rajni Kothari, that values of political development penetrate into society at various levels and by stages.

The role of the writers, artists, social workers and scientists is ever more important than the bureaucrats and politicians. They enlighten the people. Thus they preserve and promote the culture. T.S. Eliot remarked: No society without a governing elite can hope to transmit the culture it has inherited.

Karl Manheim has praised the elite by calling it "the culture' creating groups". Freidrich writes: "the elite itself sets the standards of excellence by which particular men are to be evaluated". Not only that the elite help the poor and remove their genuine grievances. In times of crisis the people look to the elite to show them the way.

Criticism of Elitism

The elite theories which had been first advocated against Marxism have been put to searching questions and found lacking.

Some of the points of criticism are:

1. Elite cannot control the whole sphere of political activity

The advocates of elite theories wrongly believe that elite can control the whole sphere of political, social and economic activity. An elite may influence one field but it cannot influence all the fields. For example, Dahl holds that economically well-off section of society cannot find any place in the sphere of education. Dahl has beautifully made a distinction between the "economic notables," "social notables" and political leaders.

2. Wealth and political position cannot be proportionate

The supporters of the elite theory wrongly hold the belief that the wealthy persons may rise to political power and control the political structure. It is not necessary that the most powerful man of the state may be also wealthiest.

Besides that it is also not certain that the wealthiest person may rise to political power. In communist countries the wealth has no role to play. Even in democratic countries like India, though the wealth has played a notable role in the elections, yet all the wealthy persons have not risen to power. Many big capitalists of India may exercise political influence upon the government directly or indirectly but they have not contested the election so far. Hence there is no proportionate relation between the two.

3. Elites are more concerned about their personal interest than the interest of the whole community

Supporters of the elite theory wrongly lead us to believe that the elites look to the interests of the whole community. In fact they never look to the interests of the whole community. In fact they never look to the interest of entire society but confine themselves to their own interests.

4. Decision-making does not lie solely in the hands of the elites

It is argued by prominent supporters of the elite theory that the decisions in the government are generally taken by the elites. When the government takes decisions, several factors influence it and not only the wishes of the elites.

5. Ideas of elites never create values

The supporters of elite theory believe that the ideas of the elites create value for the society but this is only one-sided picture. On the other hand the truth is that the elite give ideas in accordance with the values recognised by the masses because the elites can never force their values on society.

6. Elites are not cohesive, conscious and conspiratorial

The main exponents of the elite theory hold that the elites are linked by ties of common interests and they are cohesive, conscious and conspiratorial but it is not so. Friedrick says that, "It is not the class that rules but the class from which the rulers and in whose interest they exercise power." He further holds that their power is not cohesive because many rival groups hold power in the society.

7. Elites do not rule with their inherent ability

It has been held that the elites rule any country because of their inherent abilities but it is not so. The hard fact is that they have to rule the country according to the consent of the masses. Even if a small section of the people is alienated from the political system, then it may resort to protests and demonstrations which may paralyze the elite rule and the theory of the elites.

Political Elites Control Power Resources over the Masses

Luis Garrido Vergara

Luis Garrido Vergara is a PhD candidate in sociology at the University of Cambridge, Magdalene College. His research focuses on political elites in Chile and Latin America.

Elites and Social Distinction

An élite is a selected and small group of citizens and/or organizations that controls a large amount of power. Based on the social distinction with regard to other groups of lower strata (Daloz, 2010), most of these selected groups are constantly searching differentiation as well as separation from the rest of society. Normally the concept of élite is used to analyze the groups that either control or are situated at the top of societies. The creation of an élite is also the result of their evolution throughout the history of humanity. Several groups are constantly seeking different social resources in order to define their specificity.

Elites and social distinction have a long vibrant history. Since the beginning of the Greek society and the Roman Empire social status has been relevant. Whereas Greek society was mainly broken up between free people and slaves, the social structure of ancient Rome was based on property, wealth, citizenship and freedom, with a significant importance of heredity. Even though in both societies social stratification existed, in the case of the latter social status was established through objective norms (Grantt, 1978). Later on, in both Middle Ages and in Modern Times this form of distinction through the social status prevailed, and probably it could be considered as the main principle of social organization currently. Research in social sciences has emphasized the tendency of elites to persist and reproduce their power over time at "political and economic levels, potentially undermining the effectiveness

"Elites, political elites and social change in modern societies," by Luis Garrido Vergara, Faculty of Social Sciences of the University of Chile, 2013.

of institutional reforms. For instance, one specific form of élite persistence is illustrated by the existence of dynasties, a particular form of élite persistence in which a single or few family groups monopolize either political and/or economic power" (Querubin, 2011: 2).

Numerous scholars have studied the élite distinction. Through the use of a wide range of both qualitative and quantitative variables such as social status, social stratification, and local culture, amongst others, they have developed theories about its evolution and their performances in modern societies. However, a main issue has emerged with regard to the extrapolation of their predictive capabilities: "One serious problem with this topic is that social theorists have all too often been more interested in finding confirmation for their respective grand theories than in considering the various realities of distinction comparatively. Whenever they have brought empirical evidence to support their position, the main shortcoming has been extrapolation: that is the claim to provide sociological Laws on the grounds of one particular case during a given period" (Daloz, 2007: 2). According to Daloz, this "issue" has prevailed from several classical theoreticians such as Spencer, Tarde, Veblen, Simmel, Weber and Sombart to major subsequent contributions from Neo-Marxism, Functionalism and post-modern perspectives that have analyzed social distinction and emulation (Daloz, 2010). However, when sociological research started to connect social distinction with the creation of elites, a new theoretical background emerged. Pierre Bourdieu's *Distinction* (1984) is probably one of the first and most important researches focused on the relation among elites and social distinction. Under the premise of "no judgement of taste is innocent", Bourdieu attempted to analyze French bourgeoisie, its tastes and preferences. He performed a vast ethnographic study of contemporary France through the analysis of bourgeois mind. A remarkable quote, which resumes one of the main principles of distinction in social sciences according to Bourdieu's ideas, is the following:

"Principles of division, inextricably logical and sociological, function within and for the purposes of the struggle between social groups; in producing concepts, they produce groups, the very groups which produce the principles and the groups against which they are produced. What is at stake in the struggles about the meaning of the social world is power over the classificatory schemes and systems which are the basis of the representations of the groups and therefore of their mobilization and demobilization: the evocative power of an utterance which puts things in a different light (as happens, for example, when a single word, such as 'paternalism', changes the whole experience of a social relationship) or which modifies the schemes of perception, shows something else, other properties, previously unnoticed or relegated to the background (such as common interests hitherto masked by ethnic or national differences); a separative power, a distinction, diacrisis, discretio, drawing discrete units out of indivisible continuity, difference out of the undifferentiated" (Bourdieu, 1984: 479).

One of the most important contributions of this theory is the idea that social class plays a significant role in the construction of a personal identity (i.e. a person's interests). Thus, as social classes are in permanent interaction during the daily life, several "social differences" are reinforced such as the taste, which according to Bourdieu is an "aesthetic" value defined by the ruling class. These social uses of communication (Bourdieu, 1965: 1991) are also related with the relation between elites and mass (Hartmann, 2007). However, distinction is also related with other social uses and resources as power in politics and wealth in economics.

Political Elites and Social Class

A political élite is a group of people, corporations, political parties and/or any other kind of civil society organization who manage and organize government and all the manifestations of political power: "elites may defined as persons who, by virtue of their strategic locations in large or otherwise pivotal organizations and movements, are able to affect political outcomes regularly and substantially" (Higley, 2008: 3). Social class and elites are linked. Scholars have shown that one of the main aspects in the conformation of elites is given by social class patterns (Moore, 1966; Huckfeldt and Kohfeld, 1989; Lane, 2007). The most influential perspectives in sociological research historically have been provided from Marxism and Functionalism (Wright, 2005). Max Weber's sociology developed a strong theoretical framework for understanding the connection between social strata and political action in modern societies. Influenced by Marx's ideas, Weber created a theory of social stratification arguing that power could take a variety of forms in the social interplay. He emphasized the idea that besides class, there were other sources of power in modern societies, such as the status, which was defined by consumption (Weber, 1946, 1964, 1978).

Since the 1970s, a wide range of sociological empirical research has mainly focused on explaining social determinants on ruling elites. Considering topics such as social origins, type of education, socioeconomic status, social and political capital among others, several scholars have analyzed what factors explain the creation of elites as well as how they evolve in time. The main principle of this kind of research was the Weberian sociological concept of "elective affinity" (Weber, 1958), which define the association between certain variables defined by beliefs, actions, and/or unknowing or unexpected consequences of social action (Howe, 1978).

Why is it important to consider this concept of elective affinity? There is a link between the Bourdieuian theory of distinction and of the social uses of values and this Weberian concept. As political elites are constantly struggling for power and also they share social origins and interests, they are different since their origins.

Political elites are constantly controlling power resources over the mass. The elites have power over the state, the civil organization of political power. Even though they could have conflicts with the mass, which certainly can affect political decisions from "top down" to "bottom up" (Easterly, 2008), the possession of multiples forms of capital (social, cultural, economic, politic, among others) allows elites to ensure their social reproduction as well as the cultural reproduction of the ruling class.

[...]

Elites Are a Class, Not a Belief

Natalie Schmidt

Natalie Schmidt is studying engineering management systems at Columbia University. She is an editor and writer for the Pensive Post, an intercollegiate online political publication.

In the days following the election, a certain term has been used constantly by those attempting to explain Donald Trump's rise to power. Though it is more often seen in history books accompanying names like William Jennings Bryan and Huey Long, this term has now been seen on the front page of the *New York Times* and the *Wall Street Journal*.

Populism is everywhere. And not just in the United States; it's on the rise across much of Europe as well. Populism is by definition a movement of the common people against the ruling class of elites. Trump capitalized on this growing populist sentiment, especially in rural and working-class America, to fuel his campaign. He took the anger of those "deplorables" and used it to take down the epitome of political elites: Hillary Clinton.

But Trump's populism has been analyzed over and over. The more misinterpreted side of the issue is the definition of the "elites" he is so against.

Truly, it's straightforward. The ruling elites are the small group of people that have been in power either politically or financially for an extended period of time, the democratic equivalent of aristocrats. They represent the establishment, often looking to maintain the system that has kept them in power. It is important to note, however, that elites are a class, not a belief: though Trump mainly targeted Liberal elites, he went after establishment Republicans as well, such as Jeb Bush. That's because populism isn't an issue of right or left. Bernie Sanders' far-left grassroots

"Defining 'The Political Elite,'" by Natalie Schmidt, The Pensive Post, December 3, 2016. Reprinted by permission.

campaign against corporate greed and corruption in Washington is textbook populism. Similarly, the Democratic Occupy Wall Street movement directly challenged the elites of the banking industry, or in their own words, "the one percent."

But as the populism analysis of the election became more and more common, so too did confusion surrounding the definition of elites. In a recent article published by *The Pensive Post* entitled "The New Generation of Political Elite," Emma Bernstein writes that Trump has sparked the birth of a new "population of ultra left-wing political elite." She goes on to explain that this new generation she speaks of is the group of millennials who are now, due to Trump's divisive campaign, more politically active, citing their anger at Trump's rhetoric as their motivation. This generation, she claims, is everything that Trump is supposedly so against: "it is a pro-LGTBQ, feminist, anti-racist, anti-sexist, anti-fascist, and anti-hate movement."

While she is correct in noticing this increasing trend in political activism—who couldn't notice, with cities across the country shutting down streets for protests in the days following the election—the categorization of this movement as one of political "elites" is inaccurate. Just as populists are not just conservatives, elites are not just any liberals. They cannot be a large group of people that mobilized in the hours immediately following the election. They are by definition a minority, so they certainly cannot be Clinton supporters who, as we are all so often reminded, were in the *majority*, seeing as she won the popular vote. In sum, elites are solely that small class of rulers, not the common citizens across the country who subscribe to their ideology.

The classification of these new political activists as "elites" seems like a simple misnomer, but it is reflective of a greater misunderstanding many seem to have about Trump's movement. When he and his supporters attack liberal elites, they mean those in power who did nothing in the past eight years to keep the rust belt from crumbling. They mean the mainstream political culture that focused more on the urban-centered social issues than the opioid epidemic killing thousands in rural areas. Most importantly, these criticisms are not personal: Trump supporters do not inherently hate their neighbors or their coworkers—or perhaps their own millennial children—who voted for Clinton. Consequently, people should not feel as though they personally are victims of these criticisms, and therefore should not claim to be the "elites" he attacks. Yes, Trump did make some nasty comments (a certain *Access Hollywood* video comes to mind, just as one example). The people he offended personally have every right to feel that way. But while Trump's personal failings and tactless remarks should not be completely overlooked, they are not necessarily populist beliefs, and should not be used to characterize his entire campaign. Ignoring the actual issues his supporters believe in by calling them racists, sexists, xenophobes—or saying outright, "people who voted for Trump are not smart people"—is as shallow of an analysis as Trump's idea that banning all Muslim immigration could be used as a tool to stop terrorism.

This is where the real importance of this observation arises. Those who think they are the new "elite" cannot afford to oversimplify the opinions of half of the country. Admittedly, it is fantastic to see so many people, especially young people, being so passionate about this election. While protests and hashtags might not be as favorable as productive, rational discourse could be, it would be far more frightening if no one cared at all. This applies to any political event for that matter, not just this especially emotionally-charged election.

But with so many more people, particularly millennials, becoming politically active, a proper political education becomes more important than ever before. In a time dominated by social media—which is in turn dominated by misinformation—finding information from a reliable source isn't always easy, but is extremely important. But this doesn't simply mean reading the *New York Times* instead of personal statuses and questionable articles posted on Facebook; though reputable, a single source will still carry biases, presenting the readers with a narrow world view under the guise of fact. As any practiced researcher will explain, a broad range of sources, especially primary sources—direct quotes, interview transcripts, complete documents untouched by the biases of the analyzer—is essential for a real understanding of any issue. Only with a balanced, factually-based political education can one hope to come up with a complex analysis our complicated world demands.

But with great analysis comes great responsibility. In addition to the aforementioned confusion surrounding the target of Trump's criticisms, perhaps the illusion that a political education makes one an elite stems from a feeling of elitism. Yes, the point of education is to make one more knowledgeable. But any arrogance stemming from that knowledge only clouds one's judgment: looking down on the millions of people who voted for Trump and saying they are all unintelligent is not only inaccurate but pointless. First, it only deepens the divide that so enraged them in the first place. But secondly, it prevents the development of a true understanding of them, which creates a completely one-sided and shallow analysis. They might similarly misunderstand the other side of the issue—there's no denying that a rural bubble exists, just like the liberal bubble. But as a member of the politically active and educated, it is one's responsibility to understand.

I do hope young people—all people, really—continue to learn about our government, the Constitution, and current political events. The purpose of being politically active should be to use one's understanding to create effective change; we can't find any real solutions without first identifying and analyzing the real causes. But activism founded on misunderstanding and shallow interpretations is almost as detrimental as a complete lack of education; ignorance is destructive, arrogance is counterproductive. While it is too late for this election, there are still two years until midterms and four until the next presidential election; hopefully between now and then, the entire electorate—millennials, baby boomers, urbanites, rural folk—will be politically active, politically passionate, and above all else, properly politically educated.

The Caricature of the Liberal Metropolitan Elite Is Inaccurate

Ryan Shorthouse

Ryan Shorthouse is the director of the think tank Bright Blue.

Here's the life lesson I and countless others heard from our parents and teachers when we were growing up: work hard at school, go to university and chase your dream job in the big city. But these days, when you successfully do all of this, you get lambasted for being a member of the "liberal metropolitan elite."

We rightly condemn sneering and stereotyping of certain social groups: the white working-class, for example. Judging people on the basis of their social identity rather than their actions leads to discrimination and divisiveness. But we have to be consistent: you should not judge people on the basis of their socio-economic characteristics, whether they're underprivileged or privileged.

Today it seems to have become commonplace in political discourse, both from the political Left and Right, to mock and denounce the "liberal metropolitan elite." These people are basically those who live in cities, are open-minded and do well in life. We really are in trouble if we think they are a problem.

An increasing number of people live in cities in Britain. In fact, by 2030, over 90 per cent of Britons are forecast to be metropolitan. Equally, a growing majority of people in Britain have liberal attitudes on social issues. Politicians and pundits can go around in circles trying to define what liberal really means, but to most people it is associated with being tolerant of and comfortable with social diversity. Such open-mindedness is undoubtedly positive.

Moreover, denouncing the existence of an elite is anti-meritocratic. That's why it's particularly puzzling that those on the political Right are joining in this class warfare. If a member of an elite has acquired their position undeservedly, we should criticise it. If someone in the elite behaves irresponsibly or antisocially, we should speak out against it. But just being a member of the elite is not something to condemn, but to celebrate: they are people who excel in a particular field. Those on the Right should want more people to join an elite, not to shut them down.

So being a member of the "liberal metropolitan elite" is not a badge of shame. But what of the ghastly views they apparently have? Critics deem them to be snobbish, out-of-touch and excessively materialistic. The thinker David Goodhart has characterised them as "hyper-individualistic," "rootless," even "condescending." Last week, *The Daily Mail* applauded the Prime Minister for supposedly savaging "the liberal elite who sneer at ordinary Britons."

I know very few people who fit this description. Yes, many of my friends living in London are impressively ambitious, travel extensively and like nice things. But, like most people, they care deeply for their families and can't wait to get married and have children. They're proud to live in Britain, passionately civic-minded and would never look down on anybody.

Of course there are a few bad eggs, as there are in all social groups. But this caricature of the "liberal metropolitan elite" is just false.

The demonisation of this group is often expressed strongest by those on the fringes of politics who are, ironically, campaigning to become part of the elite. They blame deep-seated problems—mass immigration and poverty—on the attitudes and approaches of this elite. To note: don't trust public figures who respond to serious issues by blaming certain social groups, pitting different people against one another, rather than offering practical public policies.

Those on the extreme left and right are keen to argue that the "liberal metropolitan elite" are the beneficiaries and promoters of a bankrupt philosophy: economic and social liberalism. But the evidence is quite clear: this policy approach, of enabling free trade and free people, has led to measurable improvements in the vast majority of people's lives in recent decades. Of course there remains serious problems with certain people being left behind. They should be the priority for politicians and policymakers, with— as the Prime Minster said recently—the state playing a smarter role in supporting them. But these problems do not justify a complete rejection of this intellectual model. Nor does it mean blaming those who are successful in our society.

Yes, call me a member of the "liberal metropolitan elite." But I'm bloody proud of it.

"Metropolitan Elite" Is a Lazy Misnomer

Michael Rundell

Michael Rundell is editor in chief of the Macmillan Dictionary and director of Lexicography MasterClass.

When Jeremy Clarkson finally got the boot from the BBC, this was seen in some quarters as a victory for the metropolitan elite against the average car-loving bloke. Nothing to do with the fact that Clarkson had hospitalised one of his colleagues, then.

Language data shows that the expression "metropolitan elite" (which barely existed 20 years ago) has gone from nought to 60 in under six months, and we'll be hearing a lot more about it in this election campaign. The comment sections of online news sites (whether HuffPost, MailOnline, or the Guardian) are awash with references to a metropolitan elite hellbent on foisting its politically correct Marxist views on everyone else, and shutting down debates it doesn't approve of.

When Nigel Farage was taken to task by Leanne Wood for his comments about immigrant HIV sufferers bankrupting the NHS, the Plaid Cymru leader got the first cheer of the night in the ITV leaders' debate. But the audience must have been handpicked pinkos, because—as one online commenter explained (echoing the views of many)—"most Brits would agree with Farage, but the PC Brigade who control the way we are all supposed to think don't like what he says."

One common gripe is that "no one is allowed to talk about immigration." This will come as a surprise to anyone who scans the front pages of the Sun, Mail or Express, which rarely fail to feature a shouty headline about scrounging migrants or health tourists.

So this is the pitch: "we" are the norm, representing the views of all right-thinking Brits (aka Ukippers and/or Mail readers).

And "they"—the metropolitan elite—try to stop us saying what everyone really thinks.

But who exactly is this metropolitan elite and what are its defining characteristics? A good way of finding out about this group is to look at the adjectives typically used to describe them. The most common include smug, trendy, liberal (apparently now an insult, as it has long been in the US), patronising and (of course) politically correct. (The last one deserves a post of its own, or probably a whole book.) But the outright winner in terms of frequency has to be sneering.

A classic case was that tweet from Labour's Emily Thornberry during last year's Rochester and Strood byelection: a photo, without comment, of a house festooned with three St George's flags. The Twittersphere went crazy, while the Sun's headline was Only Here for the Sneers. To make matters worse, it turned out that Thornberry was an MP in, of all places, Islington, north London, which is not so much a physical location as a state of mind—the virtual epicentre of the sneerocracy.

But Islington is not its only hunting ground. According to the Mail's Quentin Letts, the introduction of plain cigarette packets (which enjoys cross-party support) is not about deterring young would-be smokers but owes "more to metropolitan navel-gazing than the demands of voters." The Conservatives, assumed by Letts to be against this initiative, "caved in to the pressure because they knew the policy would earn them some sympathetic coverage from the BBC—a vast silo of Hampsteadites."

Letts's target is "Hampstead socialists," while Islington is a known hotbed of Marxists. But hang on. If we are to believe Simon Heffer, the metropolitan elite is all over Notting Hill too—in the shape of top Conservatives. Heffer sees David Cameron and his chums as members of "the expensively educated metropolitan elite," and he packs no fewer than 12 references to "sneering" into his analysis of this group's attitudes. (All that sneering must get exhausting.)

If we are to believe the Conservative Woman site, this ever expanding elite comprises politicians of all three main parties, denounced as a "university educated, politically correct, metropolitan and immature elite, [which has] lost the connection with the only people who matter—the voters." (So "the voters" are assumed not to be graduates and not to be Londoners.)

This really won't wash. An elite is by definition a tiny group that wields power out of all proportion to its size—like the investment bankers who crashed the global economy, for example, though for some reason they get away with it. But anyone who has a degree or lives in London or might vote for a party other than the Tories and Ukip is supposed to be part of a minuscule unrepresentative cabal.

Another commenter, sneering (yes!) at Leanne Wood's intervention in the leaders' debate, opined on Guido Fawkes' site: "In reality, the majority of the British people agree with Farage and Ukip." No they don't. Ukip is currently polling around 14%. That's a small minority, not "most people." Ukip supporters have as much right to be represented as anyone else, but they don't have the right to claim they represent "the average person."

There's always a temptation to believe that everyone else thinks the same way we do, unless there's something weird about them. But it's a delusion. The whole "metropolitan elite" schtick, which seems to have a range of mutually exclusive definitions, is just a lazy substitute for thinking, and a convenient way of marginalising anyone you don't agree with.

CHAPTER 3

Do Special Interest Groups Keep the Political Elite in Check?

Overview: Interest Groups and Elite Theories Explain the Driving Forces in Politics

The University of Toledo

Interest Group Theory

Interest Group Theory believes that many different interests compete to control government policy, and that their conflicting interests can balance out each other to provide good government. It is a very American theory that is popular with political scientists. It fits well with economic principles such as Adam Smith. Leading advocates are James Madison (*Federalist No. 10),* Alexis de Tocqueville (1824), Bentley (1905), David Truman (1950), and Robert Dahl (*Who Governs?).* Its advantages are that it is comparatively neutral as to values and explains process. The theory is also called pluralism because there are many groups.

An interest group may be defined as an organized body of individuals who share policy goal and try to influence policy, for example the AFL CIO, the American Bankers Association, the American Medical Association, NRA, the Diabetes Association, the Children's Defense Fund and the NAACP. It differs from a political party in that it does not try to win office. The power of an interest groups comes from its: 1. size (number of members), 2. wealth, 3. organizational strength, 4. leadership, 5. access to decision makers and 6. internal cohesion. Groups form when a disturbance occurs and people come together to resist change. The leader is a policy entrepreneur like Ralph Nader, Lois Gibbs, Clara Barton, or David Brower. Interest groups often lobby in Washington, where their techniques are direct, grass roots, information campaigns and coalition building. Groups sometimes compete with each other, and sometimes cooperate.

The tenets of the theory are that the task of the political system is to manage group conflict by establishing the rules of the game, arranging compromises, enacting the deals into law, enforcing the laws and adjudicating them. Government is like a referee calling the balls and strikes. Public policy is only a temporary equilibrium. Adherents believe that government is held together by: 1. latent group which supports the system, 2. overlapping membership in different groups, 3. checks and balances of group competition and 4. agenda building. Both the group leaders and political scientist believe that situation will remain fluid permanently; no one group will have a permanent victory.

The recent campaign finance reform law is premised on interest group theory. It assumes that many groups are too powerful because they can raise money to donate to politicians, therefore the law restricts them. Critics often agree that the groups can spend a lot of money, but believe the law will merely make the donations harder to track. Like James Madison, they believe the solution is to play one group against another. The idea that "money talks" in this direct fashion is a form of group theory.

Elite Theory

Elite theory believes that a wealthy elite runs the United States. The economic elite consists of the same people as the political elite (wealth equals power). The elite exerts power downward on the masses. A large minority of political scientists believe the theory. Leading advocates are Karl Marx, Gaetano Mosca, Robert Michels ("the iron law of oligarchy"), and C. Wright Mills (*The Power Elite*).

The theory maintains that very rich families are in power, people such as the Rockefellers, the Fords, and the Pews. They tend to live in the Northeast and attend exclusive prep schools and Ivy League universities. They tend to belong to mainline Protestant churches and they marry one another. Often members of the elite do not occupy governmental positions themselves, but depend on elected and appointed officials who do their work for them. It takes two or three generations of wealth to arrive in the elite. New members of elite are thoroughly socialized by the time they arrive at the top. Power flows downward making it democratic theory in reverse. The elite shares a consensus on the importance of private property, limited government, individual liberty and the fact that change should be incremental rather than revolutionary. As demonstrated in many charities, the elite may be may be public regarding, displaying a sense of noblesse oblige. On the other hand, big foundations like the Rockefeller Brothers, Ford, Pew, Johnson, etc. have the added benefit of keeping control of stock in the hands of the family and avoiding taxes. The elite manipulates the masses by exploiting symbols such as charity or elections. Philanthropy reduces the threat that the masses will demand that money be seized from the wealthy. The power of money is latent and takes a long time to have its effect. It is not the direct "money talks" of group theory.

Although few political scientists who believe the elite theory consider it good for democracy, they consider it to be an accurate view of reality. It does have the advantage of reducing conflict due to elite consensus. Two presidents make an interesting contrast. George H. W. Bush (Senior) came from an old New England family that gained its wealth in banking. He attended Andover School and Yale University. Bill Clinton came from a working class family in Arkansas. Rising out of the masses, he attended a mid-range prestige university, Georgetown, and an Ivy League law school, Yale. He also won a Rhodes Scholarship to study at Oxford University in England. He married Hillary Rodham, who had her undergraduate degree from one of the Seven Sisters and was the daughter of a Chicago businessman. Elite theorists consider Bush to be a member of the elite and Clinton as an official who was recruited to serve the elite. George W. Bush (Junior) is not quite as pure an example of the elite as his father, although his own mother was also from an old wealthy New England family. He was raised in Texas even though he was born in Connecticut. Like his father, he attended Andover and Yale.

Several Categories of Special Interest Groups Contribute to the Shape of American Politics

R. Allen Hays

R. Allen Hays is an emeritus professor of political science at the University of Northern Iowa. He has written extensively about the federal government and urban housing.

Interest groups are one important mechanism through which citizens in the United States make their ideas, needs, and views known to elected officials. Citizens can usually find an interest group that focuses on their concerns, no matter how specialized they may be. Directories of American voluntary associations reveal the incredible variety of reasons why citizens band together. The Gale Research, Inc., Encyclopedia of Associations is widely regarded as one of the most comprehensive lists. Not all of these groups are politically active, but a great many try to influence public policy.

Both the formal structure and the informal traditions of American politics provide fertile ground for interest groups. One feature of the American system that enhances their influence is the relative weakness of U.S. political parties, which stems, in part, from the separation of powers between the executive and legislative branches. In a parliamentary system such as Great Britain, where the prime minister's hold on office depends on majority support in Parliament, parties exert considerable control over legislators and, as a consequence, over policy making. In contrast, elections of the U.S. president and Congress are politically separate events, even when held at the same time. Each legislator must construct a winning coalition in his or her state or district, and the nature of these coalitions is quite different from the majority coalition that the successful presidential candidate assembles. Clear evidence for

"The Role of Interest Groups," by R. Allen Hays. Accessed at https://www.ait.org.tw/infousa/zhtw/docs/demopaper/dmpaper9.html. Reprinted by permission of the author.

this is the fact that Congress and the presidency have been in the control of opposing parties most of the time since World War II. As a consequence, neither Democrats nor Republicans are invariably bound to support the positions of their party's president or their party's electoral platform. Weak party loyalty enhances interest-group influence, both during elections, when their financial support can be critical, and afterwards, when groups that supported the winning candidate become closely involved in policy making.

A second feature of the system that encourages interest groups is the decentralization of political power to states and localities, known as the federal system, or "federalism." Citizen associations often get started at the state and local levels, later combining into national organizations. Decentralization thus encourages a greater variety of interest groups. It also further weakens the party system, because the social and economic diversity of the 50 states make strict party discipline difficult.

In addition, a strong, independent judiciary in the American system enhances the power of interest groups. U.S. courts often rule on issues that, in other democratic polities, would be under the control of the legislature or bureaucracy. Thus, interest groups can utilize litigation to achieve policy objectives that they cannot obtain through legislative action. For example, in the early 1950s, court victories by the National Association for the Advancement of Colored People (NAACP) created the first cracks in American racial segregation, years before a Congress dominated by Southerners in key positions was willing to act.

Finally, the American tradition of virtually unlimited freedom of speech, press, and assembly means that nearly any point of view expressed by an interest group, no matter how radical, is permitted a public airing. To be sure, the increasing centralization of the media since World War II has made it more difficult for groups with fringe views to gain a serious hearing. However, this centralizing trend has been partially counteracted by the open access granted to groups on the Internet. On the whole, the American free speech and free press traditions, which offer numerous opportunities to publicize societal problems and lay out positions on public policy, encourage group formation.

The Universe of Interest Groups

Before 1970, the typical American textbook on interest groups devoted most of its pages to three categories: business, labor, and agriculture. Since then, the interest-group universe has become much more complicated. Agricultural groups have lost influence due to the declining number of farmers in the United States. In addition, many new groups that fit none of these categories have emerged.

Business

Most scholars would agree that business plays a central role in American politics. Major corporations carry the prestige of being important players in the U.S. economy. Because elected officials are held accountable for the nation's economic performance, they often fear anti-business policies will harm that performance.

Yet, business also utilizes direct levers of influence. Large multinational corporations bring vast resources to bear on their political goals. They are usually members of multiple trade associations, which represent an entire industry's views in the political process. Corporations also support "umbrella" groups, such as the National Association of Manufacturers and the U.S. Chamber of Commerce, that speak for the whole business community. Finally, individual companies directly lobby legislators, and they funnel millions of dollars in campaign contributions to the candidates they favor.

Labor unions

Labor unions grew slowly in the early part of the 20th century, but they gained a significant place in the American political system in the 1930s. The National Labor Relations Act protected collective bargaining and enabled unions to grow much faster. They reached a peak membership of 35 percent of the labor force in the 1950s. However, in the 1960s, union membership began to decline toward its current level of approximately 15 percent of the working population, and the political power of unions declined along with their economic power. The reasons for this decline in union membership, too complex to discuss in detail here, lie in the changing nature of the global economy, and the shift in the United States from a manufacturing-based economy to one more service-oriented. Unions, however, still exert considerable clout when they focus their energies on an election or an issue.

Professional associations

Another important type of interest group is the association of professionals. Groups like the American Medical Association and the American Bar Association focus on the collective interests, values, and status of their profession. Less powerful, but nonetheless well organized, are professionals in the public sector. Virtually every specialty within state and local governments has its own national organization. In housing policy, for example, groups include the National Association of Housing and Redevelopment Officials, the National Council of State Housing Agencies, and the Council of Large Public Housing Authorities. Such groups are restricted from partisan activities by state and federal laws. However, they testify before Congress on issues affecting their programs, and they organize their members to speak with representatives from their own states or districts. Since low-income clients of public programs rarely organize themselves into interest groups that are influential at the national level, these associations of service providers are an important voice for the poor in the American political process.

Intergovernmental groups

A related category consists of interest groups representing units of state and local government, lobbying for their interests on the national level. While these groups have no official role in the U.S. federal system that divides authority among national, state, and local governments, they function much as other interest groups do. That is, they present the views of their members to Congress and the administration and make the case for their positions in the media. The National Governors' Association (NGA) and the National Conference of State Legislatures represent state officials, for example. Since state governors have direct administrative and political responsibility for carrying out social welfare programs mandated by the federal government, the NGA in particular has been influential in helping members of Congress draft social welfare legislation. The general institutional interests of counties are represented by the National Association of Counties, and those of cities by the National League of Cities and the U.S. Conference of Mayors.

Public interest groups

The type of interest group experiencing the most rapid growth since 1970 is the "public interest group." Political scientist Jeffrey Berry defines a public interest group as one that supports goals that are not of direct material benefit to its members but rather express their values pertaining to society as a whole. The first public interest groups were spawned by the civil rights, women's rights, and environmental movements of the 1960s. Supporters of these causes often went through an evolution over time that transferred the expression of their views from street protest to organized action within the political system. Later, public interest groups mobilized on new issues, such as the rights of the disabled, prevention of child abuse or domestic violence, and gay/lesbian rights. These groups have also been major advocates for programs benefiting the poor. Some leading groups of this type include the National Low Income Housing Coalition, the Children's Defense Fund, and Public Citizen (the group led by consumer activist Ralph Nader).

Public interest groups generally lack the financial resources of business groups. While the issues they champion often enjoy considerable public support according to opinion polls, few have mass memberships. One reason for this is that the intangible nature of their goals contributes to the "free rider" problem—that is, an individual can benefit from an interest group's efforts without being a member, or at least without being heavily involved. Nevertheless, they use their expertise and information-gathering efforts to raise issues that no other groups are addressing. Initially, most public interest groups were on the left of the political spectrum. However, in recent years conservatives have organized their own groups, largely in response to the perceived liberal shift of public policy in the 1960s and 1970s. Among leading public interest groups in this category are the National Taxpayer's Union and Concerned Women for America. Conservative think tanks such as the Heritage Foundation may also function as interest groups, as their research tends to support the conservative world-view. The same could, perhaps, be said about the Urban Institute on the liberal side.

These domestic public interest groups resemble the Non-Governmental Organizations (NGOs) that have sprung up on the international scene since the 1980s. In fact, some American groups have close ties with international NGOs. In both cases, support comes from citizens concerned about a general social issue, rather than immediate economic interests.

Limits on Interest-group Effectiveness

As this brief survey suggests, there are a great variety of interest groups on the American political scene; a large body of research indicates that their effectiveness in making the views of their members heard varies considerably. The reasons for this disparity lie in how a group employs its chief political resources: membership, cohesion/intensity, money, and information.

Number and Cohesion of Members

It would seem logical to assume that interest groups with a large base of support in the population would be the most influential. Elected officials champion the policies advocated by significant majorities in opinion polling, because they want to add the large number of potential voters supporting these positions to their winning coalitions. However, several factors complicate this picture.

It is true that millions of citizens belong to interest groups and that some, such as the environmentalist Sierra Club and the AFL/CIO, the labor organization, are quite large. However, a closer look shows that most mass-membership groups enroll only a small fraction of their potential supporters. For example, polls show substantial majorities of Americans in favor of strong environmental regulations. These supporters constitute a pool of millions of potential members for environmental interest groups. However, even the largest environmental groups claim memberships of under one million. This relatively small number of members is in keeping with the overall principle that the number of citizens who join interest groups is a small fraction of the U.S. population.

The late economist Mancur Olson advanced the most plausible explanation for this phenomenon. He argued that the achievement of a policy goal by an interest group is, in economic terms, a "public good." That is, the benefits of a group's success are enjoyed by those who agree with a group's position, whether or not they actually join the group. Thus, if whales are saved from extinction, one can derive satisfaction from their existence, even if one never paid dues to a "save the whales" interest group. It is true, of course, that if no one contributes, the group won't exist. However, in large groups the marginal contribution of each new member is small. Therefore, while thousands of supporters will join, many others will not join the group or make a full commitment; they will become "free riders," i.e., enjoying the benefits while others actively participate and pay.

Another serious problem faced by a mass-membership group is translating citizen support for the group into votes for candidates that support its goals. Voting is a complex act, involving multiple motivations and influences: the candidate's personality, party loyalty, and a range of issues. Voting studies show that many voters are not fully aware of the policy positions taken by candidates they support. As a result, it is often difficult for a group to show that the voting choices of its supporters are primarily motivated by its particular issues. Groups that can convince candidates of their voting power become feared and respected. For example, the

National Rifle Association (NRA), which opposes gun control laws, has convinced legislators that its members will vote for or against them solely on this issue. Therefore, the NRA wields influence far out of proportion to its numbers, even though most Americans favor stronger gun control laws.

Because of the difficulties of mobilizing mass memberships, it is not surprising that smaller cohesive groups with more intensity of feeling often exercise influence far greater than their numbers might suggest. First, the smaller the group, the larger the marginal contribution of each member, so that "free riders" are reduced. Secondly, until the advent of the Internet, communication among members was much easier in smaller groups, thus making mobilization much easier. If these advantages of smaller size are reinforced by its members having a large stake in policy outcomes, then even a small group may become very powerful.

Money

The importance of money in American politics has increased in recent years, due to the escalating costs of political campaigns. Existing laws limiting campaign contributions have gaps in them, and, many elected officials from both parties are reluctant to support changes in the current system that might give some advantage to their opponents. Interest groups that are most influential in national elections generally make voluntary contributions to candidates totaling in the hundreds of thousands of dollars.

In addition, considerable financial resources are needed to maintain a presence in Washington between elections. A group needs a professional staff to influence legislation affecting its interests, in addition to the staff needed to communicate with its members and to offer them services. Groups without a steady Washington presence cannot exert the behind-the-scenes influence on the details of legislation that is the hallmark of a successful interest group.

Money also interacts with the factors of membership and cohesion. In order to overcome the free rider problem, groups must attract "policy entrepreneurs"—that is, individuals who seek material, professional, or ideological rewards from organizing a successful group. To do so, the group's potential membership must have sufficient surplus resources to provide a promising organizational base. This need for a surplus creates an income floor, below which potential groups are unlikely to be organized. For this reason, relatively few groups directly represent the poor.

Above this floor, however, the role of resources becomes more complex. In the abstract, one might argue that a group with 1,000,000 members who each contribute $5 could raise as much money ($5,000,000) as a group with 10,000 members who can contribute $500 each. It is only when one considers the free rider problem, plus the high costs of communicating with a large membership, that the true disadvantage of the larger group becomes apparent.

Another factor affecting a group's mobilization of resources is whether its membership consists of individual citizens or of other organizations. Many powerful interest groups are, in fact, organizations of organizations. This includes trade associations, professional associations, and groups representing public and nonprofit service providers. A group composed of other organizations has fewer entities to mobilize, yet it can still claim to represent the thousands of people affiliated with those entities. In addition, its members can use organizational resources, rather than personal financial resources, to support it.

Information

Next to a committed membership and money, information is the most powerful resource that an interest group can possess. Information is exchanged in several ways. First, information passes from interest groups to decision-makers. Groups often have technical knowledge that legislators lack, and they are eager to educate lawmakers on the issues they care about. It's true that the information they provide generally comes with a bias that reinforces the group's interests. Legislators are well aware of the bias, but may still find this information useful. One of the main advantages of a continuous presence in Washington is the opportunity to provide information to lawmakers at key points in the decision-making process.

Second, information flows from the legislative and executive branches to interest groups. Their staffers track legislative proposals, thus becoming aware of the most propitious times to try to influence the legislative process. Their informal contacts with congressional staff provide opportunities to testify at hearings and to mobilize their group's members when a crucial vote is near. Through this process, they learn which actors are most powerful and what strategies will gain their support. On occasion, they can obtain a modification to the detailed language of a bill in Congress that will affect its impact.

Finally, interest groups exchange information with members and with other citizens. They may conduct an investigation or commission a study that dramatizes a problem. If they attract sufficient media attention, legislators feel pressure to respond. They also solicit information from their members, and inform them about upcoming decisions. On most legislation, only a small number of private citizens contact their legislators. Therefore, 200 letters orchestrated by a group can seem like a blizzard of mail.

The rapid growth of the Internet during the last five years has radically reduced the cost of communication among large numbers of citizens. Most interest groups now have Web pages, and many use e-mail both to communicate with members and as a means for their members to communicate with decision-makers. However, the medium is so new that groups are still learning how best to utilize it, and it is too early to tell exactly how much influence it will have on the process of interest-group influence.

One recent example of such influence was the use of certain conservative Web sites to circulate negative information about former President Bill Clinton, some of it accurate and some of it grossly distorted or fabricated. This probably helped keep the momentum for Clinton's impeachment going, although a majority of Americans still opposed it. Unless large economic actors figure out a way to control Internet access, and thus increase its cost, the new medium is likely to have a democratizing influence on political dialogue. Conversely, it is possible that the Internet may also encourage the fragmentation of citizens into small, electronically linked groups who isolate themselves within increasingly bizarre world views.

Toward More Effective Public Interest Groups

For these reasons the preferences of smaller, more cohesive, better financed groups win out, more often than not, over the preferences of groups representing larger numbers of citizens. And particularistic interests frequently prevail over the more general interests of what one might call the larger public. The proliferation of public interest groups in recent years does, however, make the interest-group system as a whole more representative of the diversity of opinions among Americans. And public interest groups are often able to score victories over seemingly more powerful, better-financed opponents. At the end of the day, though, elected officials know that it takes money to win votes. Many times mass-based interest groups cannot reliably deliver the votes of their members, but trade associations and individual corporations can reliably deliver the dollars that candidates need to buy television advertising.

A crucial missing element in many public interest groups is the lack of genuine grassroots political organization. These groups typically consist of a small staff, supported by thousands of members whose only link to the group is periodic financial contributions. This structure is in contrast to earlier forms of mass political organization, in which national movements were built from smaller, face-to-face local organizations. With the exception of a small number of activists, members of modern groups rarely meet face to face.

Recent observers of American society have become increasingly concerned with a decline in community involvement by citizens.

This decline applies to nonpolitical, as well as political organizations. Many causes have been advanced for this phenomenon: the isolating effects of television; the increase in dual-career and single-parent families where adults have little leisure time; and the cynicism generated by media-dominated campaigns that focus on personalities and scandals, rather than meaningful issues.

Whatever the causes of this decline, an interest group that could effectively mobilize people through local, grassroots chapters would be in a powerful position politically. It would develop a steady membership base that would be less expensive to reach because of established channels of communication. By supplementing national lobbying with direct local contacts with candidates and office holders, it could convincingly argue that its members will vote based on group issues. It would truly be a mass movement, rather than a small elite, funded by passive supporters.

However, the obstacles to creating such a group are formidable. A large initial infusion of money would be necessary to support local organizing campaigns. It would also have to overcome the American tendency to separate local from national issues. Finally, many citizens would have to be wooed from their tendency to focus on issues raised by the national media at the expense of face-to-face exchange with their neighbors.

A hallmark of a democratic society is that it allows citizens to create alternative political resources that they can mobilize when they believe private economic actors or government officials violate their interests. In that sense, organized interest groups play a fundamental role; they help citizens more effectively utilize the resources they have: voting, free speech, assembly, and the judicial process.

The Policy Preferences of Special Interests Must Align with Those of the General Public

James Swift

James Swift is a writer and reporter whose work has been published by the Juvenile Justice Information Exchange, Youth Today, the Center for Public Integrity, and the Journal of Blacks in Higher Education.

The argument presented by Martin Gilens and Benjamin Page, the authors of a new paper set to be published in the fall 2014 edition of Perspectives on Politics, is straight-forward: In the United States today, C. Wright Mills' "The Power Elite" may prove a more accurate explanation of what influences public policy than Tocqueville's "Democracy in America."

In "Testing Theories of American Politics: Elites, Interest Groups and Average Citizens," Gilens, of Princeton University, and Page, of Northwestern University, examine four theoretical "traditions"—majoritarian electoral democracy, economic elite domination, majoritarian pluralism and biased pluralism—and the sway of ordinary citizens, interests groups and economic powerhouses on public policy.

"A great deal of empirical research speaks to the policy influence of one or another set of actors, but until recently it has not been possible to test these contrasting theoretical predictions against each other within a single statistical model," the paper reads.

Using a data set containing key variable measures for more than 1,700 policy issues, the authors of the paper said the results "provide substantial support" for economic elite domination and biased pluralism theories—leaving the long-held, and to some long-cherished, theories of majoritarian pluralism and majoritarian electoral democracy nearly out of the political equation altogether.

The Methodology

For the study, Gilens and Page looked at four actors; the median U.S. voter as an individual, economic elites, mass-based organizations and business-oriented interest groups and industries. Defining majoritarian pluralism as a system "in which the interests of all citizens are more or less equally represented," the findings from the paper clearly vouch for the antithesis—biased pluralism, "in which corporations, business associations and professional groups predominate"—as the more fitting description of contemporary U.S. politics.

For the study, 1,779 public policy cases—stemming from national surveys collected between 1981 and 2002—were used to measure the influence of popular opinion on public policy. "The included policies are not restricted to the narrow Washington 'policy agenda,'" the paper reads. "At the same time—since they were seen as worth asking poll questions about—they tend to concern matters of relatively high salience, which is plausible that average citizens may have real opinions and may exert some political influence."

Using quadratic logistic regression techniques based on original survey data, researchers then estimated the opinions of poor (bottom 10 percentile), middle-income (50th percentile) and affluent (top 10 percentile) respondents. Responses from middle income respondents were used as proxies for the majoritarian electoral democracy theory, while responses from affluent survey-takers were used as proxies for the economic elite domination theory.

To meter the impact of biased pluralism in the political arena, researchers used a net interest group alignment measure, with the policy stances of interest groups listed in Fortune's "Power 25" annual rankings serving as proxies.

"For each of the 1,779 instances of proposed policy change, Gilens and his assistants drew upon multiple sources to code all engaged interest groups as 'strongly favorable,' 'somewhat favorable,' 'somewhat unfavorable,' or 'strongly unfavorable' to the change," the paper reads. "He then combined the numbers of groups on each side of a given issue, weighting 'somewhat' favorable or somewhat unfavorable positions at half the magnitude of 'strongly' favorable or strongly unfavorable positions."

To draw distinctions between net group interest alignments, researchers then assessed business and professional groups separately from other mass-based interest groups, thus pitting groups like the American Hospital Association, oil companies and the National Federation of Independent Business up against organizations like the National Rifle Association, the AARP and United Auto Workers.

For the project, the dependent variable would be whether or not the policy changes preferred by each income percentile or organization type were adopted within four years of the survey questions being circulated.

The Results

The findings are unmistakable; per Gilens' and Page's report, proposed policy changes with strong support from economic elites are much likelier to be adopted than policy changes with strong support from median-income earners. Similarly, the paper found business and professional interest groups to be likelier to see their requested policy changes take place than other mass-based interest organizations.

"Multivariate analysis indicates that economic elites and organized groups representing business interests have substantial independent impacts on U.S. government policy," the authors of the paper state, "while average citizens and mass-based interest groups have little or no independent influence."

However, the public policy stance of median-income Americans may not be all that different from the public policy stances of the upper echelon. According to the paper, the public policy preferences of average Americans registered a .78 correlation with the public policy preferences of the economic elites.

"Rather often," the paper reads, "average citizens and affluent citizens, our proxy for economic elites, want the same things."

Conversely, the stances of interest groups largely differed from the public policy stances of most median-income citizens. "Taking all interest groups together, the index of net interest group alignment correlates only a non-significant .04 with average citizens' preferences," the paper reads. "This casts grave doubt on David Truman's and others' argument that organized interest groups tend to do a good job of representing the population as a whole."

Even "mass-based" interest group stances do not seem to vibe with the political leanings of middle-income Americans, with non-business organizations of the like scoring a statistically significant, although "very modest," .12 correlation with the political stances of average Americans. By comparison, business-oriented interest groups fared even worse, posting a -.10 correlation with median income citizen ideals.

Mass-based and business interests groups did not appear to sync up with the political stances of economic elites, either—a finding researchers considered surprising.

"[This] may reflect profit-making motives among business as contrasted with broader ideological views among elite individuals," the paper said. "For example, economic elites tend to prefer lower levels of government spending on practically everything, while business groups and specific industries frequently lobby for spending in areas from which they stand to gain."

As a result of their findings, the authors suggests that modern state of U.S. "democracy" is best described as an amalgamation of competing economic elitist and organized business-based interests. Meanwhile, the overall impact of "median voters," researchers said, has dropped to almost zero when considered as an independent public policy factor.

"The chief predictions of pure theories of majoritarian electoral democracy can be decisively rejected," the authors of the paper declare. "Not only do ordinary citizens not have uniquely substantial power over policy decisions; they have little or no independent influence on policy at all."

The "Death" of Democracy?

In examining 1,779 policy cases, researchers found that when narrow public majorities rallied for policy changes, those changes came about roughly 30 percent of the time. However, even with gargantuan pro-change majorities—with as many as four-fifths of the general public favoring policy shifts—the American majority only saw those changes come about 43 percent of the time. According to Gilens, those percentages simply reflect how often economic elites or business interests sync up with the policy preferences of the general public.

With their data demonstrating the massive clout of business-interests and economic heavyweights, do the researchers themselves believe that America can no longer be considered a nation where "majority rule" is still a reality?

Despite media outlets like BBC, U.S. News and Slate explicitly using the term in write-ups on his report, Gilens said it's a bit too early to describe contemporary U.S. politics as as an oligarchical system.

"'Oligarchy' brings to mind this image of a very small number of extremely wealthy individuals pulling the strings," Gilens told Uncommon Journalism. "I don't think that's the situation in America today. We have a somewhat larger group of people who have the interests and the means to influence what our government does and we have a very poorly functioning democracy, in terms of the degree to which that ability to shape policy outcomes is widespread, but I don't think it's so narrowly constrained as to justify the term."

However, he said the outcomes of his study remain concerning for ordinary citizens.

"The situation for working Americans is impacted in very fundamental ways by the political decisions that they have little influence over," Gilens said. "We've seen, for example, how, over the last two decades, the middle class has stagnated economically, and we've seen how the growth in our economy has more and more been narrowly confined to the people at the top…these are things that really affect people's lives."

Furthermore, he said his findings speak to the "very fundamental nature" of the type of society and government the United States promotes. "To me, living in a society where the majority of citizens have such little ability to shape what their government does, it's extremely distressing," Gilens said. "And I don't think it's what most Americans believe America should be, and maybe not even what many of them think America is."

While his findings demonstrate noticeable overlap between the public policy wants of average Americans and the affluent, Gilens does not believe the economic elite can be considered a "voice" for the middle class.

"I think there's a distinction between getting what you want because some powerful other group or individual happens to share your preferences, and getting what you want because you actually have a say in the political system," Gilens said. "Sure, you could say it would be even worse if there was less overlap between what middle class Americans and what economic elites prefer…but it's certainly not the kind of system that I think most people think about when they think about what it means to be a democracy."

Middle class Americans, he said, shouldn't have to depend on the agreement of the "powerful other" in order to see their political needs and wants addressed by government. However, with economic inequality increasing overall over the last few decades, Gilens said it is unlikely that "economic elite domination" will be supplanted as the nation's primary political model anytime soon.

Nonetheless, he believes there are ways for the middle class to address the issue.

"On the other hand, to the extent that both average Americans become concerned enough to really work for reform, and engage onto the issue of who has say over government policymaking, and to the extent that middle class Americans can find allies among the well to do," Gilens concluded "one can imagine the situation would improve."

Referencing the recent outcome of *McCutcheon v. Federal Election Commission*, a Supreme Court case that did away with aggregate limits on individual election cycle contributions, Gilens said campaign finance reform could be a pivotal first step towards leveling the political playing field.

"There are proposals for ways of sort of reforming campaign finance laws, consistent with recent Supreme Court decisions, that could fundamentally alter the role of money in the political system," Gilens said. "And that, I think, is the change that will be required to bring about a whole range of policy changes that middle income Americans might prefer to see."

The Interests of the Wealthy Dominate the Political System

Douglas J. Amy

Douglas J. Amy is professor of politics at Mount Holyoke College. He has published a number of books, including Real Choices/ New Voices: How Proportional Representation Elections Could Revitalize American Democracy *and* Government Is Good: An Unapologetic Defense of a Vital Institution.

While it is crucial to acknowledge all that is right with American government, we must not turn a blind eye to what is wrong with it. Although government on the whole is good, there are things wrong with government—things that need to be fixed. And fixing those problems is necessary if we are to revive Americans' support for government. The better we can make government, the more we can expect citizens to oppose efforts to undermine this vital institution.

Readers of the other articles on this site might have gotten the impression that I was suggesting that there are no serious problems with American government. But my argument has not been that there is nothing wrong this institution—only that it is not what *conservatives* say it is. It is simply not the case that government grossly overtaxes us, or that bureaucracies are incredibly wasteful, or that Big Brother is constantly threatening our freedoms. What is wrong is something altogether different—and something more disturbing. The main fault of our government is that it is not as democratic as it should be. We have what some have called a "deficit of democracy."

The problem is that American government is now increasingly responsive to special interests and not the public interest. This is

Douglas J. Amy, "What is Really Wrong with Government," Government is Good, An Unapologetic Defense of a Vital Institution (2011), http://www.governmentisgood.com/articles.php?aid=23. Reprinted by permission.

why many people are frustrated and disappointed with our political system. Instead of a democracy where all citizens have an equal say in the governing process, some organizations and individuals have a disproportionate and unfair influence over what the government does. The result is that the power and greed of the few too often win out over the needs of the many.

This problem is getting worse and it is increasingly limiting how good government can be in the United States. The less responsive a government is to its citizens, the less liable it is to act in the public interest. The more it favors the interests of the few over the interests of the many, the less likely it is to do all the good things it could do. Most of the substantial achievements of government described in this book have occurred because it was reacting to demands made by the public to deal with serious social and economic problems. So if we want our government to live up to its potential as a force for good in society, we need it to be as democratic as it can be. That is why it is crucial to understand exactly why our democracy is falling short, and what can be done to fix that.

The Public's Disappointment with American Democracy

While many politicians ignore our democratic deficit, most Americans are painfully aware of it. Surveys find that they are increasingly concerned that their democratic government is not working for them the way that it should. In the last ten years, the number of people who say that "public officials don't care about what people like me think" has ranged from 50% to 75%—up from 36% forty years ago. Polls show that many in the public also have a very clear sense of who really is influencing what government does. A clear majority now says that "the government is run by a few big interests looking out only for themselves."[1]

This perception—that government is working for the few, not the many—is part of what fuels public hostility toward politicians and government in general. A 2000 survey found that over 60%

of respondents cited the undue influence of special interests as a reason for not trusting government.[2] The less democratic a government is, the less legitimate its actions are and the more alienated the public becomes. In this book, I have been arguing that much of modern cynicism about government is unfounded —but in this case, it is not. It makes a great deal of sense to be cynical about a government which seems to consistently favor special interests over the public interest. When people feel that they have little say over what government does and see that their government is not working democratically, it is only natural to be distrustful of that institution.

The Real Problem: The Mal-Distribution of Private Power

But while it is natural to lay the blame for our unresponsive public institutions at the doorstep of politicians and the government itself —this is a mistake. Undemocratic government is just the symptom. The ultimate source of this political illness lies in society at large —in the private sector. The real problem is that private economic power—primarily money—is not distributed equally among all citizens. Some people and organizations have very large financial resources that they can then turn into political influence. Private economic power too easily becomes public political power, and this is what is undermining the conditions of political equality that are so essential to a well-functioning democracy.

For a society to be truly democratic, political power must be shared by all—it must be distributed relatively equally among all citizens. All citizens must have a voice in determining government policy. This principle is what lies at the heart of a democracy. And this is what Lincoln was getting at when he described democratic government as being "of the people, by the people, and for the people." Americans understand this principle very well. In surveys, as many as ninety-five percent of them endorse the idea that "every citizen should have an equal chance to influence government policy."[3]

If we all have the same basic amount of political power, then government will respond to what most people want—and its actions are more likely to be in the public interest. That is why elections are so crucial to democracies—why they are defining characteristics of democracies. Ideally in elections, we all have the same exact amount of power: our one vote. A suburbanite does not have more votes than a farmer, and a rich person can't vote more often than a poor one. So the vote is the ultimate form of equal political power. And if it were the only form of political power, our democracy would not be in so much trouble.

But the vote is just one among many other sources of political power. And many of these other sources are located in the private sector where they are distributed very unequally. The result is that instead of being responsive to average Americans, our government is primarily reacting to a powerful elite. And this is undermining the promise of American democracy. The political dangers of this situation were recently highlighted by a task force of distinguished political scientists put together by the American Political Science Association. They issued a disturbing report entitled: *American Democracy in an Age of Rising Inequality.*[4] They concluded that despite efforts to ensure that all citizens have an equal voice in our political system, increasing levels of economic inequality in the United States are threatening this democratic ideal:

> Generations of Americans have worked to equalize citizen voice across lines of income, race, and gender. Today, however, the voices of Americans citizens are raised and heard unequally. The privileged participate more than others and are increasingly well organized to press their demands on government. Public officials, in turn, are much more responsive to the privileged than to average citizens and the least affluent. Citizens of lower and moderate incomes speak in a whisper that is lost on the ears of inattentive government officials, while the advantaged roar with a clarity and consistency that policy-makers readily hear and routinely follow.[5]

The Worsening Problem

The report goes on to conclude that this problem is getting worse. "Recent analysis indicates that the government has become less responsive than it was several decades ago and that it is [now] particularly attentive to the views of the affluent and business leaders."[6] Two developments over the past thirty years have increased political inequality and the disconnection between politicians and the average American. First, the financial disparities between individual Americans—which were large to begin with —have been increasing. The benefits of our growing economy have been accruing disproportionately to those who are already well-off. Not only has the gap between the rich and the poor been widening, but so has the gap between the rich and the traditional white-collar and blue-collar middle class. Here are some disturbing facts about the high level of economic inequality in America and how it is getting worse, not better.[7]

- Income is distributed highly unequally in this country. Over half of all income (50.3%) goes to the top fifth income class of families. The income going to the top 5% of richest families (21.7%) is twice the combined income of the bottom 40% –the 110 million Americans living on low and moderate incomes.
- Income inequality is getting worse. Between 1947 and 1979, the income for all classes of American grew at relatively the same rate. But more recently, between 1979 and 2009, the incomes for the richest 5% of families grew by a whopping 73%; and incomes for the richest 20% by an impressive 49%. But the increases for the bottom 60% of families have been pitiful in comparison—their gains were a meager 7%.
- In 1979, the average income for the top 5% was 11 times that of the lowest 20%. In 2006, that ratio had grown to 20 times —another indication of the growing mal-distribution of economic rewards.
- In 1965, CEOs made 24 times the wages of the typical worker. By 2007 that ratio had ballooned to 275 time the earnings of those workers.

- Meanwhile the value of the minimum wage continues to decline. In the late 1960s, the minimum wage was worth 50% of average worker's hourly wage. By 2007, it was worth just 33.5% of the average worker's wage.
- The inequality in wealth among Americans is even more extreme. In 2004, the top fifth richest families owned a staggering 84.7% of all the wealth of the country. The next 40% owned only 15.1% and the poorest 40% owned less than 1%. The last time the distribution of wealth in this country was this skewed was in the 1920s, right before the Great Depression.
- The top 20% of wealthy Americans own 90.7% of the stock. The bottom 80% owns a mere 9.4%. And 77% of the increased values of stocks between 1989 and 2004 went to a very few Americans—just the wealthiest 10% of households.
- Many believe that the increasing popularity of IRAs and mutual funds has given everyone in America of piece of the wealth pie—but that is wrong. The bottom half of Americans own less than 1% of the value of mutual funds, and a mere 3.3% of individual retirement accounts.
- Upward mobility, the ability to move up the economic ladder, is declining in America. Since the 1970s, fewer Americans have been able to move up and more of those at the top have stayed there.
- Not surprisingly, given all these figures, the U.S. has the highest level of economic inequality among developed countries. We are the worst in both income inequality and wealth inequality. To make matters worse, we also have the highest poverty rate and the most children in poverty.

These facts and figures graphically illustrate the growing economic divide among Americans. This situation is not simply disturbing for moral reasons, but also because of the corrosive impacts it is having on the operation of our democracy.

The second development in the private sector that is undermining political equality and democracy is the political mobilization of the corporate community. In the 1970s, the business community was reeling from legislative defeats from environmentalists, labor, and consumer protection groups. They were increasingly concerned about the costs of new regulations. Corporations that had previously been largely apolitical realized that they had to begin to devote more resources to their political efforts. And so corporate interests launched a very well-funded and well-planned campaign to increase their political power – pouring hundreds of millions of dollars into political campaigns, advocacy advertising, think-tanks, etc. This process has been well chronicled by Jacob Hacker and Paul Pierson in their insightful book, *Winner-Take-All-Politics: How Washington Made the Rich Richer—and Turned Its Back on the Middle Class.*[8]

The result has been that today business has become by far the most powerful organized interest in the United States – greatly outdistancing other large groups such environmentalists, the Christian Right, and the elderly. Labor used to be the traditional liberal counter-balance to business, but its membership has been in steady decline for decades and its political influence in Washington is now minimal. So when large multi-national businesses choose to mobilize their enormous economic resources to influence public policy, no other group in society is able to match those efforts. This doesn't mean that business wins every political fight, but it does mean that business almost always has the political advantage.So that is the basic problem: financial inequality is the rule in the private sector, and that has been creating more and more political inequality in the public sector. A coalition of the well-off—wealthy individuals and prosperous companies—now exerts an enormous and disproportionate amount of power in our governmental system. Let's look at exactly how they manage to pull this off.

How Private Power Becomes Public Power

There are a number of troubling ways that private power is being turned into public power. Typically it involves large amounts of money. Money is the handiest and most versatile form of power because it can buy so many different forms of political influence. It can buy advantages for political candidates, fund massive lobbying efforts, and produce volumes of politically useful information and analysis. Let's consider each of these things in turn.

Financing Campaigns

Winning office today requires a lot of money, so campaign contributions now play a very crucial role in the election process. For instance, contributions help determine who can run for office in the first place. As the APSA report explains: "To win a seat in national office, the incumbent and challenger usually have to win the support of funders before they go before voters. The effect can be to discourage certain kinds of challengers who, for instance, promote egalitarian policies that would redistribute resources from affluent campaign contributors."[9] In other words, candidates who don't support the priorities of wealthy contributors often can't amass the resources necessary to make a viable run for office.

More importantly, donations can buy candidates many advantages—like larger campaign staffs, more high-priced consultants, more media time, and better ads—in their pursuit of voter support. Candidates with more money simply have a much better chance of attracting voters and beating their opponents. Contributions to campaigns, then, are an extremely important form of political influence—they play a significant role in determining who wins office. But this influence is wielded disproportionately by affluent individuals and organizations.

For instance, the campaign donations of political action committees come primarily from organizations that are financially well-off. Corporate and industry trade PACS now far outnumber and out-donate all other interest groups. In the 2008 elections, for instance, these business-oriented PACs outnumbered Labor

PACs by almost ten to one and outspent them by four to one —$321 million to $73 million.[10] Or consider the uphill battle faced by grassroots interest groups like environmentalists. In 2008, environmental PACs contributed $811,000 to various races. But the PACs for several industries that often fight against increased environmental regulations (energy and natural resources, construction, chemical, and automotive) contributed 50 times that amount—$40 million.[11] It's not hard to guess which groups are more able to help elect their preferred candidates.

This corporate dominance of campaign funding was made even worse by a 2010 Supreme Court ruling that overturned the longstanding ban on corporations spending directly on political campaigns. They are now able to spend as much money as they want to defeat candidates they oppose and to threaten elected officials who don't share their political priorities.

Supporters of our current financing system like to point out that many contributions come from individuals—not PACs or corporations. This seems to suggest that it is the average American voter who is financing most campaigns. Nothing could be farther from the truth. There is a huge class bias to these donations. In 2002, 83% of all the itemized donations to campaigns were given by less than one-half of one percent of the U.S. population. And almost three-fourths of these total donations ($1.9 billion) came from a relatively small group of well-off Americans who could afford to donate $2,300 or more.[12] This is not public participation —this is rich people's participation.

Recently, some have argued that the emergence of groups like MoveOn.org has signaled a switch to a more grassroots and democratic approach to funding campaigns. And in 2008, that organization did manage to raise $38 million through the use of the internet and local meetings. But in reality, this figure is a drop in the bucket compared to the $2.2 *billion* spent by campaigns that year.

So campaign finance is a perfect example of how the concentration of money in the private sector leads to imbalances of power in the public sector. This situation directly undermines the democratic nature of elections. Who gets elected should be determined by the voters, not by well-heeled donors whose contributions give their preferred candidates large and unfair advantages over others. Wealthy individuals and organizations should not have more say over who get elected than the rest of us.

These skewed donations not only affect whose candidates win office, but the behavior of political parties as well. The Democratic and Republican parties are supposed to be rivals that represent very different constituencies. But both have become increasing dependent on wealthy donors and business PACs. This has pushed the Democratic Party farther to the right and has made it less responsive to many of its less affluent constituents, such as workers, minorities, and the poor. Not only elections, but parties are becoming less democratic as well.

Lobbying

Another major source of political influence is lobbying—organized efforts to sway the decisions of policymakers. Lobbying largely determines whose problems and concerns get the attention of policymakers, and whose arguments get a better hearing. In the last thirty years, more and more groups have established lobbying offices in Washington—groups representing environmentalists, gays, the elderly, farmers, consumers, and so on. This gives the appearance of a fair and healthy competition between all interests. But this is only an illusion.

First, not all lobbying organizations are born equal, and the competition between them does not take place on a level playing field. Again, money is what makes the difference. Some lobbies have much larger and more reliable sources of funds, and this tilts this political process in favor of these more wealthy interests. Interests with more money can, for instance, create more lobbying groups to promote their cause. It is hardly a coincidence that the majority of organizations lobbying in Washington, D.C. are corporations. Many these firms also enjoy multiple avenues of representation.

Most businesses, for instance, belong to trade groups who also lobby in Washington. General Electric belongs to over 80 trade organizations—most of which also have lobbying arms. If you add together all the corporations, trade groups, and well-off professional organizations (doctors, lawyers, etc.), they make up over a staggering 75% of all lobbying efforts. In contrast, public interest organizations like environmentalists, consumer groups, and civic organizations make up only 4% of lobbying groups. Even more stunning, if you add together unions, civil rights groups, the elderly, women, educational groups, farmers, and veterans, they make up less than 10% of lobbying efforts.[13]

Not only does more money fund more lobbying efforts, it also pays for larger offices with more staff and better support. More money also buys more effective and more expensive lobbyists—particularly retired members of Congress who are still friendly with their former colleagues on the hill. Money also makes is easier from some lobbyists to get direct access to policymakers. Members of Congress are very busy and can't see everyone who knocks on their door. But lobbyists with direct access to policymakers have a much better ability to make their case. Studies show that who gets in and how much time they get is often directly related to the size of their campaign contributions.[14]

Given all this, it is little wonder that two of our leading scholars on interest groups activity, Kay Schlozman and John Tierney, have concluded that the lobbying process "is skewed in favor of groups representing the well-off, especially business, and against groups favoring broad public interests and the disadvantaged."[15]

The Power of Ideas

Another way that well-off interests wield political influence is by affecting the way other people look at policy issues. Ideas, information, and analysis are important sources of political persuasion and power. They influence how we look at the world —how we see political issues, what problems are considered important, how political debates are framed, and which policies are considered justified. They are a vital form of intellectual ammunition in political fights. But here again, the competition in this area is not fair. Ideas, information and analysis are commodities—and those interests with more money can pay experts to produce more of these commodities. So this is yet another way that advantages in private financial resources are translated into advantages in political power. It is another way that the voices of affluent interests drown out the voices of average Americans.

Another of my writings, "The Anti-Government Campaign," chronicles the ability of wealthy families and businesses to funnel billions of dollars into foundations, think-tanks, and universities —the main organizations that produce and promote the work of political intellectuals and policy experts. These intellectual investments produce two kinds of political payoffs. First, these efforts are very useful in lobbying policymakers. Members of Congress can only specialize in a few policy areas, and so they are often dependent on outside sources of information to inform their votes on many complex issues. Well-funded—largely conservative —think-tanks are more than happy to oblige. They provide a steady stream of detailed studies, expert testimony, and Congressional briefings that greatly aid the lobbying efforts of well-heeled interests like big businesses.

The other target of this intellectual barrage is public opinion. There is a concerted effort to shape the public's ideas about what is desirable politically. If the public can be convinced, for instance, that "what is good for business is good for America," this provides increased legitimacy for those seeking to roll-back regulations and cut business taxes. So a great deal of money has been spent on creating a sophisticated communications system that constantly promotes the ideas of conservative intellectuals and think-tanks to the public. Materials are sent to reporters on a daily basis and frequent guest commentators are provided to network news shows. Information and analysis are also funneled through right-wing political pundits like Rush Limbaugh, Sean Hannity and Fred Barnes who then disseminate these ideas through conservative cable news channels like Fox News, right-wing internet sites, and hundreds of national and local radio talk shows.

Vastly Unequal Citizens

So what does all of this add up to? Incredible imbalances in private and public power and a political playing field that is hugely uneven. A typical non-unionized worker has her one vote, but few other ways to influence policy. Her measly $25 campaign donation is lost in the avalanche of special interest contributions. She might write a letter to her Congressperson, but it will likely be drowned out by the organized letter-writing campaigns of large lobbies. In contrast, for a corporate executive, his vote is his least important political tool. He can have much more influence by donating thousands of dollars to political action committees as well as thousands more in individual donations to specific candidates—all working to increase the election chances of his favorite politicians. And his economic interests are also much better represented in the policymaking process by the many well-healed organizations that lobby for his firm and industry. Finally, our executive is more likely to have his political and policy ideas pitched to Congress by think-tank experts and espoused to the public by media pundits. So here we have two Americans, two citizens who are supposed to be political equals, but who have vastly different amounts of power. This maldistribution of political power cannot help but have a corrosive effect on our democracy.

The Result: Policies by and for Affluent Special Interests

These imbalances of power produce a clear bias in the political system toward the interests of affluent individuals and businesses. Policymakers are more apt to listen to these interests and design policies with them in mind. Several recent studies have sought to gauge the political clout that various economic classes had over the decisions of politicians. One found that "senators are vastly more responsive to the views of affluent constituents than to the constituents of modest means."[16] In fact, if the poor and working class support a particular policy that means that senators are actually *less* likely to vote for it. Another empirical study of public opinion and policy found that "the American political system is a great deal more responsive to the preferences of the rich than to the preferences of the poor."[17] Finally, a study found that even if a majority of Americans supports a new policy, it doesn't stand a good chance of becoming law unless it is also supported the well-off.[18] Hardly surprising, but very disturbing none the less.

It is not hard to find specific policy examples of this political tilt toward the well-off. Tax policy is exhibit number one. In recent years, the public has not been citing tax cuts as one of their highest priorities. In fact, polls reveal that most Americans would now rather forgo more tax cuts and spend that money on areas like education and health care. And yet for over a decade, the Republican-dominated Congress continued to put tax cuts high on their legislative agenda. Such behavior by policymakers makes much more sense when it is understood that these cuts have disproportionately favored the rich and businesses – the very interests who have the dominant powerbase in our political system. It is hardly a coincidence that in the first year after the 2003 tax cuts, households making over $1 million were granted a gift of nearly $100,000 in tax cuts, while the average tax cut for a middle-class family was a paltry $217. Nor is it just a matter of luck that Congressional tax policies—under both Democrats and Republicans—have reduced the share of federal taxes paid by businesses from 20% of total federal revenue in 1975 to a mere 7% in 2003.[19] One of the most blatant examples of elite power occurred in 2010, when the Republican Party refused to allow the extension of unemployment benefits to millions of jobless Americans unless the Democrats agreed to extend the Bush tax cuts for the rich. These are just a few examples of how tax policy has produced immediate and large pay-offs for the money that affluent interests have invested in buying political influence.

This current imbalance of financial and political power not only helps to explain what Congress *does*, but also what it *does not do*. It sheds light on why Congress is so slow to act on some serious problems—especially problems that are not of particular concern to the moneyed interests wielding the most power. Consider, for instance, the problem of unemployment. The recent deep recession has left record numbers of people without jobs. And millions who want full time work can only find part time jobs. But in the face of this unemployment crisis, Congress has largely sat on its hands and has done little to promote the creation of more jobs. Largely this is because the suffering of American workers is of little interest to the well-moneyed interests that dominate in our political system.

Or take health care policy. For many decades now, our health care crisis has been growing. Over 47 million Americans had no medical insurance. Employers were cutting back on coverage for their workers. Many middle-class families were being financially pressed by increasing medical costs. Financially strapped state governments began limiting access to Medicaid for many people living in poverty. The quality of medical care was highly uneven and we compared poorly to most other Western countries in terms of life expectancy and infant mortality. And yet in the face of all of this, Congress was reluctant to act in any vigorous or concerted way. For decades we remained the only Western democracy that did not provide some form of universal health care for its citizens. And all this despite consistent public support for major health care reform. By almost a two-to-one margin, Americans said they would rather scrap the current employer-based insurance system and replace it with a government program that would provide coverage for everyone. Three-quarters of Americans said that access to health care should be a right—not something available only to those who can afford it. And 67% said they would even be willing to pay more in taxes to make this universal coverage a reality.[20] Still, until the election of President Obama, most members of Congress – both Democrats and Republicans—adamantly refused to promote such a universal plan. Why was that the case?

The answer had to do with the imbalance of political power that has been described here. First, health care reform was not a high priority for those who are well-off in society—they had no problem affording the best medical care. More importantly, there were powerful special interests who benefited from the current system and who diligently worked against any attempts to create a universal health insurance system. A sociologist, Jill Qaudagno, has written an insightful book about this problem entitled *One Nation Uninsured: Why the U.S. Has No National Health Insurance.*[21] She showed how powerful private interests were able to block every effort in Congress to move toward a national health care program. In the 1960s, it was primarily physicians who torpedoed the attempt. In recent years, it has been insurance companies and employers. And even when health care reform was finally passed in 2010, the Republicans and their health care industry allies were able to block the most promising and wide reaching reform proposals, such as the single-payer government plan that has proved so successful in other Western democracies.

Needed: More Power to the People

It hasn't always been the case that wealthy interests have so successfully dominated our political system. There have been times in our past when Congress rose up to pass broad-based policies that greatly extended economic equality, economic security, and economic opportunity among all citizens—legislation such as Social Security in the 1930s, the G. I. Bill in the 1940s, and Medicare in the 1960s. These egalitarian policies improved the lives of virtually all American families and are widely recognized as political and moral highpoints in American politics. But today these kinds of progressive bills would face a huge uphill battle in Washington, even with the Democrats in charge. Such efforts would be quickly attacked by powerful special interests, and condemned by most conservatives as expensive and wasteful "big government" programs that would only raise taxes. The shift in political power that has taken place toward well-off individuals and corporations has made it very difficult to pass these kinds of egalitarian policies.

It is this shift in power, not a shift in public opinion, which has created the rightward swing toward more inegalitarian policies. Most Americans still support a broadly egalitarian political agenda—higher minimum wages, more help for the poor, most affordable higher education, and so on. What has changed is not public opinion, but the distribution of power. Most Americans back more government spending on health care and education, and more regulations that protect workers and the environment. Social programs, taxes, and regulations have been cut not because the public has demanded it, but because those with the most power have demanded it. As the APSA report concluded: "Interest groups and money are tools wielded disproportionately by a small segment of American citizens to enact policies that concentrate benefits on them and to block egalitarian policies..." That, in a nutshell, is the alarming policy result of the shift in political power that is undermining democracy in the United States.

Some people believe that electing more liberal politicians, like Barack Obama, will help to solve this deficit of democracy. It can't hurt. But a change in elected leaders can only do so much to address the undemocratic tendencies that have become deeply embedded in our economic and political systems. If we are to really remedy these problems, we need more basic reforms.

Endnotes

1. Lawrence R. Jacobs and Theda Skocpol, eds., *Inequality and American Democracy* (New York: Russell Sage Foundation, 2005) p. 8.
2. Ibid. p. 8.
3. Ibid. p. 25.
4. Task Force on Inequality and American Democracy, "American Democracy in an Age of Rising Inequality," American Political Science Association, 2004. This was later published in book form: Lawrence R. Jacobs and Theda Skocpol, eds., *Inequality and American Democracy* (New York: Russell Sage Foundation, 2005).
5. *Inequality and American Democracy*, p. 1.
6. *Inequality and American Democracy*, p. 117.
7. Most of these economic facts and figures came from Economic Policy Institute, *The State of Working America*, January 2006-2007. http://www.epinet.org/content.cfm/books_swa2006; and Inequality.Org, "How Unequal Are We, Anyway?" November, 2008. http://www.inequality.org/facts.html

8. Jacob Hacker and Paul Pierson, *Winner-Take-All-Politics: How Washington Made the Rich Richer – and Turned Its Back on the Middle Class.* New York: Simon and Schuster, 2010.

9. *Inequality and American Democracy,* p. 115.

10. These figures come from the website Open Secrets.Org, http://www.opensecrets.org

11. Open Secrets.Org.

12. Open Secrets.Org.

13. Kay L. Schlozman and John T. Tierney, *Organized Interests and American Democracy.* New York: Harper and Row, 1986, pp. 67-68.

14. *Inequality and American Democracy,* p. 116.

15. Schlozman and Tierney, *Organized Interests and American Democracy,* p. 66.

16. *Inequality and American Democracy,* p. 127.

17. *Inequality and American Democracy,* p. 127.

18. Martin Gilens, "Inequality and Democratic Responsiveness," *Public Opinion Quarterly* 69, no.5 (2005): 778-96/.

19. *Statistical Abstract of the United States, 2004 ed. (Washington, DC: U.S. Printing Office, 2004), p. 300.*

20. This poll figures can be found in Ruy Teixeira, "Public Opinion and Universal Health Care," The Emerging Democratic Majority web site, September 16, 2005. *http://www.emergingdemocraticmajorityweblog.com/donkeyrising/archives/001291.php*

21. Jill Quadango, *One Nation Uninsured: Why the U.S. Has No National Health Insurance* (Oxford: Oxford University Press, 2005).

Money Is the Most Influential Factor in Elections

Rachel Alexander

Rachel Alexander is the editor of Intellectual Conservative and a senior editor at the Stream. She contributes to outlets including Townhall, Selous Foundation for Public Policy Research, the Christian Post, and Right Wing News.

E lections are not about choosing the most qualified, experienced, or intelligent candidates. The single most influential factor in an election is money. Television ads and campaign mailers are still the most effective way to influence races, and the candidates and issue advocacy organizations with the most money to spend in these areas generally win. Whether the money is given directly to a candidate, or is spent independently of a candidate is irrelevant, it all has the same effect. Who can forget the effect the Swift Boat Veterans for Truth ads had on the presidential race between George W. Bush and John Kerry.

The biggest contributors to political campaigns come from the left. Many of these organizations are closely tied to government. Unions only exist in some states by force of government regulation. This connection has gotten even more powerful this year, with the rise of the government employees' union as the top contributor to political campaigns. The American Federation of State, County, and Municipal Employees (AFSCME) spent $87.5 million this year to help Democrats. AFSCME is ranked as the third biggest contributor to campaigns cumulatively over the past 20 years, with 98% of its money going to Democrats.

What is most disturbing about this is that government is now indirectly the largest special interest group influencing elections. How did this union get to be so powerful? Through gradual

"Which Special Interest Groups Are Pouring the Most Money into Elections?" by Rachel Alexander, Townhall.com, November 1, 2010. Reprinted by permission.

expansion of the size of government. Now that AFSCME has become this powerful, it has enormous influence ensuring that government remains bloated and continues expanding. An example of its influence: Federal employees now make double the amount of money as their counterparts in the private sector, and have been awarded higher pay and benefit increases than those counterparts for the past nine years in a row. Federal employee salaries alone have grown 33% faster than inflation since 2000. Their private sector counterparts have seen their total compensation grow by only 8.8% in that same period. Federal employee compensation increased despite the recent downturn in the economy. Since larger government favors Democrats, the rise of AFSCME means bad news for Republicans in the future.

The second biggest contributor to elections this year was the U.S. Chamber of Commerce. Although the Chamber has traditionally been associated with right-leaning candidates, this is changing. In 2008, 20% of the Chamber's campaign contributions went to Democrats. This year that percentage will probably increase, as the Chamber has endorsed several Democrats – including Democrats like incumbent Congressman Harry Mitchell in Arizona, whose record could hardly be qualified as moderate. Mitchell voted for TARP, the stimulus, Obamacare, and cardcheck. He has tried to portray himself as a moderate Blue Dog Democrat by voting against Democrat leadership on silly administrative procedures.

The Chamber is also supporting Democrat Senatorial candidate Joe Manchin in West Virginia, and spent $1.9 million to help Democrat Congressmen Glenn Nye in Virginia, Travis Childers in Mississippi, Bobby Bright in Alabama, Jim Marshall of Georgia, and Frank Kratovil of Maryland. The reason for the Chamber's support of Democrat candidates is no doubt due to those candidates' support for the federal TARP bailouts. Some of the top corporate contributors to the Chamber or its foundation were recipients of the bailouts, like Goldman Sachs and AIG, whose charity contributed to the Chamber's foundation. The Chamber has traditionally been a reliable advocate for fiscal conservativeness, but appears to be shifting away from that now, much like many of the companies it represents.

Of the 15 largest contributors to political parties and Congressional candidates since 1989, 12 contributed almost exclusively to Democrats, three gave mostly equally to both parties—and none gave mostly to Republicans. AT&T was the top contributor, contributing slightly more to Republicans than Democrats, for a total of $45 million. In 2008, however, AT&T contributed more to Democrats. ActBlue came in a close second, contributing $43 million over the past 20 years all to Democrats. Others in the top 15 that contributed mostly to Democrats are AFSCME, Goldman Sachs, International Brotherhood of Electrical Workers, American Association for Justice, National Education Association, Laborers Union, Carpenters and Joiners Union, Services Employee International Union (SEIU), Teamsters Union, American Federation of Teachers, and Communications Workers of America. The National Association of Realtors and Citigroup rounded out the top 15, contributing mostly equally to both Republicans and Democrats.

Some of those same groups also invested heavily in independent expenditures to affect political campaigns. The only organizations on the right that made the top 50 were the NRA and the Club for Growth. Approximately half of the top 50 were unions. SEIU spent more money than any other organization over the past 20 years on independent expenditures, $69 million. The National Rifle Association came in second, spending $56 million over the past 20 years. AFSCME came in third, spending $52 million. The next biggest spenders in the top 50 were the AFL-CIO with $39 million, the National Association of Realtors with $33 million, and the National Education Association with $30 million. Other far left groups in the top 50 include EMILY's List, Human Rights Campaign, and the American Association for Justice.

Due to the Citizens United U.S. Supreme Court decision this past January, which struck down restrictions on corporations from spending money to influence political campaigns, there may be some new large corporate independent expenditures this year. The expenditures could favor the left, since the make up of the Board of Directors from the largest 20 corporations are comprised of either board members on the left or a range of viewpoints across the political spectrum; there are no boards comprised of board members on the right.

However, if contributions to Republicans and Democrats in the past by the PACs and employees of corporations are any measure, there may be some hope for Republicans. The top 10 corporate contributors in the past two election cycles include a few companies that generally give more to Republicans, like Wal-Mart. In addition, corporate giving tends to fluctuate based on which party is in power or is anticipated to be in power. Although some industries generally favor one party or another (oil and gas favors Republicans, lawyers favor Democrats), most companies started shifting the bulk of their support back to Republicans this year.

The old saying "money talks" is live and well and today in political campaigns. Attempts to regulate it through failed campaign finance reform legislation have only succeeded in slightly revising the paths used to push the money through. The usual suspects are still behind most of the big money—left-leaning organizations. The rise of big special interests representing government will further ensure that more left-leaning candidates get elected. Conservatives can only hope that more corporations take advantage of Citizens United and vote based on fiscal economic principles, not short-sighted bailout mindsets.

CHAPTER 4

Do Average Americans Have an Opportunity to Be Heard?

Overview: The Average American vs. the Political Elites

Martin Maximino

Martin Maximino is a writer at Journalist's Resource.

P ublic policy in the United States is shaped by a wide variety of forces, from polls and election results to interest groups and institutions, both formal and informal. In addition to political parties, the influence of diverse and sometimes antagonistic political forces has been widely acknowledged by policymakers and evidenced by scholars, and journalists. In recent years concerns have been growing that deep-pocketed donors now play an unprecedented role in American politics—concerns supported by 2013 research from Harvard and the University of Sydney that found that for election integrity, the U.S. ranked 26th out of 66 countries analyzed.

The question of who shapes public policies and under what conditions is a critical one, particularly in the context of declining voter turnout. From both a theoretical and practical point of view, it is important to understand if voters still have the possibility of providing meaningful input into public policies, or if the government bypasses citizens in favor of economic elites and interest groups with strong fundraising and organizational capacity.

A 2014 study published in Perspectives on Politics, "Testing Theories of American Politics: Elites, Interest Groups, and Average Citizens," analyzes the relative influence of political actors on policymaking. The researchers sought to better understand the impact of elites, interest groups and voters on the passing of public policies. The authors, Martin Gilens of Princeton and Benjamin Page of Northwestern, based their research on a database of voters' and interest groups' positions on 1,779 issues between 1981 and 2002, and how those positions were or weren't reflected in policy decisions.

The scholars use the data to examine four theoretical conceptions of how American politics works and the degree of influence that parties have on the decision-making process: (1) majoritarian electoral democracy, in which average citizens lead the decision-making process; (2) economic-elite domination; (2) majoritarian pluralism, in which mass-based interest groups provide the driving force; and (4) biased pluralism, where the opinions of business-oriented interest groups weigh most heavily.

The study's key findings include:

- Compared to economic elites, average voters have a low to nonexistent influence on public policies. "Not only do ordinary citizens not have uniquely substantial power over policy decisions, they have little or no independent influence on policy at all," the authors conclude.

- In cases where citizens obtained their desired policy outcome, it was in fact due to the influence of elites rather than the citizens themselves: "Ordinary citizens might often be observed to 'win' (that is, to get their preferred policy outcomes) even if they had no independent effect whatsoever on policy making, if elites (with whom they often agree) actually prevail."

- Regardless of whether a small minority or a large majority of American citizens support a policy, the probability of policy change is nearly the same—approximately 30%.

- A proposed policy change with low support among economically elite Americans is adopted only about 18% of the time, while a proposed change with high support is adopted about 45% of the time.

- Interest groups have a substantial impact on public policy. When mass-based and business-oriented interest groups oppose a policy, the probability of its being enacted is only 16%, rising to 47% when they're strongly favorable. "On the

1,357 proposed policy changes for which at least one interest group was coded as favoring or opposing change, in only 36% of the cases did most groups favor change, while in 55% of the cases most groups opposed change."

- Overall, business-oriented groups have almost twice the influence of mass-based groups.

- While the popular belief is that professional associations and interest groups serve to aggregate and organize average citizens' interests, the data do not support this. The preferences of average citizens are positively and highly correlated with the preferences of economic elites but not with those of interest groups. Except for labor unions and the AARP, interest groups do not tend to favor the same policies as average citizens. In fact, some groups' positions are negatively correlated with the opinion of the average American, as in the case of gun owners.

"The central point that emerges from our research is that economic elites and organized groups representing business interests have substantial independent impacts on U.S. government policy, while mass-based interest groups and average citizens have little or no independent influence," the scholars conclude, providing "substantial support" for the theories of economic-elite domination and biased pluralism.

Related research: A 2010 study by Jacob S. Hacker of Yale and Paul Pierson of University of California, Berkeley, "Winner-Take-All Politics: Public Policy, Political Organization and the Precipitous Rise of Top Incomes in the United States," examines structural and political explanations for rising inequality. Further, a 2014 literature review, "Advancing the Empirical Research on Lobbying," written by John M. de Figueiredo of Duke and Brian Kelleher Richter of the University of Texas, Austin, provides an overview of leading scholarship and suggests promising social science methods and new data sources. They find that lobbying expenditures at the federal level are approximately five times those of political action committee (PAC) campaign contributions. For instance, in 2012, organized interest groups spent $3.5 billion annually lobbying the federal government, compared to approximately $1.55 billion in campaign contributions from PACs and other organizations over the two-year 2011-2012 election cycle.

Efforts to Foster Change, However Small, Can Make a Difference

Jennifer Earl

Jennifer Earl is a professor of sociology at the University of Arizona, as well as a Public Voices fellow. She has won several awards for her work.

I n 2013, an online petition persuaded a national organization representing high school coaches to develop materials to educate coaches about sexual assault and how they could help reduce assaults by their athletes. Online petitions have changed decisions by major corporations (ask Bank of America about its debit card fees) and affected decisions on policies as diverse as those related to survivors of sexual assault and local photography permitting requirements. Organizing and participating in these campaigns has also been personally meaningful to many.

But, a nostalgia for 1960s activism leads many to assume that "real" protest only happens on the street. Critics assume that classic social movement tactics such as rallies and demonstrations represent the only effective model for collectively pressing for change. Putting your body on the line and doing that collectively for decades is viewed as the only way "people power" works. Engaging online in "slacktivism" is a waste, making what cultural commentator Malcolm Gladwell has called "small change."

This amounts to a debate over the "right way" to protest. And it's bound to heat up: The election of Donald Trump is pushing many people who have not previously engaged in activism to look for ways to get involved; others are redoubling their efforts. People have a range of possible responses, including doing nothing,

"'Slacktivism' that works: 'Small changes' matter," by Jennifer Earl, The Conversation, December 16, 2016. https://theconversation.com/slacktivism-that-works-small-changes-matter-69271. Licensed under CC BY-ND 4.0.

using online connections to mobilize and publicize support and protesting in the streets—or some combination of tactics.

As a social movement scholar and someone who believes we should leverage all assets in a challenge, I know that much social good can come from mass involvement—and research shows that includes online activism. The key to understanding the promise of what I prefer to call "flash activism" is considering the bigger picture, which includes all those people who care but are at risk of doing nothing.

Most People Are Apathetic

Social movement scholars have known for decades that most people, even if they agree with an idea, don't take action to support it. For most people upset by a policy decision or a disturbing news event, the default is not to protest in the streets, but rather to watch others as they do. Getting to the point where someone acts as part of a group is a milestone in itself.

Decades of research show that people will be more willing to engage in activism that is easy, and less costly – emotionally, physically, or financially. For example, more than a million people used social media to "check in" at the Standing Rock Reservation, center of the Dakota Access Pipeline protests. Far fewer people – just a few thousand—have traveled to the North Dakota camps to brave the arriving winter weather and risk arrest.

Once people are primed to act, it's important not to discourage them from taking that step, however small. Preliminary findings from my team's current research suggest that people just beginning to explore activism can be disheartened by being criticized for doing something wrong. Part of the reason people volunteer is to feel good about themselves and effective about changing the world. Shaming them for making "small change" is a way to reduce numbers of protesters, not to increase them. Shaming can also create a legacy of political inactivity: Turning kids off from involvement now could encourage decades of disengagement.

"Success" Takes Many Forms

"Flash activism," the label I prefer for online protest forms such as online petition, can be effective at influencing targets in specific circumstances. Think of a flash flood, where the debilitating rush of involvement overwhelms a system. Numbers matter. Whether you are a high school coach, Bank of America, the Obama administration or a local council member, an overwhelming flood of signatures, emails and phone calls can be quite persuasive.

Further, all that 1960s-era street-style protest is effective only in certain circumstances. Research shows it can be very good at bringing attention to topics that should be on the public or policymakers' agenda. But historically protests are less successful at changing entrenched opinions. For instance, once you have an opinion about abortion access, it is fairly difficult for movements to get people to change their views. And, while the protests we are so nostalgic for sometimes succeeded, they also often fail where policy change is concerned.

The Glass Can Be Half-Full

Online protest is easy, nearly cost-free in democratic nations, and can help drive positive social change. In addition, flash activism can help build stronger movements in the future. If current activists view online support as an asset, rather than with resentment because it is different from "traditional" methods, they can mobilize vast numbers of people.

Take, for example, the "Kony 2012" viral video campaign calling for the arrest of indicted war criminal Joseph Kony. Some hated the campaign; others highlighted its ability to draw attention to an issue many thought Americans wouldn't care about. Think about the possibilities. Would Planned Parenthood be unhappy if 100 million Americans watched a persuasive short movie on abortion rights as civil rights today, and shared it with friends? Would the effort "matter"; would it help drive the direction of the public conversation about abortion?

And flash activism isn't necessarily just a one-time game of numbers; MoveOn showed that with a big enough membership base, you could mobilize large numbers repeatedly. People who participate in one online action may join future efforts, or even broaden their involvement in activism. For example, kids who engage in politics online often do other political activities as well.

Many Hands Make Light Work

Critics often worry that valuing flash activism will "water down" the meaning of activism. But that misses the point and is counterproductive. The goal of activism is social change, not nostalgia or activism for activism's sake. Most people who participate in flash activism would not have done more—rather, they would have done nothing at all.

Worse yet, when people denigrate flash activism, they are driving away potential allies. Critics of online efforts no doubt know that not everyone is willing to march or rally—but they miss the important potential for others to take actions that support and actually result in change.

Scholars and advocates alike should stop asking if flash activism matters. We should also stop assuming that offline protest always succeeds. Instead, we should seek out the best ways to achieve specific goals. Sometimes the answer will be an online petition, sometimes it will be civil disobedience and sometimes it will be both—or something else entirely.

The real key for grassroots social change is to engage as many people as possible. That will require flexibility on how engagement occurs. If people want larger and more effective social movements, they should be working to find ways to include everyone who will do anything, not upholding an artificial standard of who is a "real activist" and who is not.

Protest Can Rejuvenate Democracy

Jeremy David Bendik-Keymer

Jeremy David Bendik-Keymer is a professor in ethics at Case Western Reserve University.

With the new administration beginning, many people might want to know how to resist it. The inauguration week includes many protests against Donald Trump's values—from the Women's March on Washington to the #J20 Art Strike. What should we aim for as we head into protests?

As a reflective citizen and a practitioner of philosophy, I am hopeful about the power of protest. I see our time as challenging us to ensure that protests take democratic form. When we do, protest rejuvenates democracy.

A "Hollowing Out"

On the face of it, our democratic values are in trouble. In new work on democracy, the political theorist Wendy Brown argues that neoliberalism is "hollowing out" democracy without our realizing it, like rot inside a tree.

Neoliberalism is a form of thinking in which human values are reduced to capitalist market values, especially financial ones. Brown develops the concept from Foucault's lectures on the governance of human populations. Foucault asks how people are managed as a people. His answer is that a new way of thinking sets in from the government on down to individual lives.

For example, in Citizens United, Supreme Court Justice Anthony Kennedy characterized political speech as a "marketplace" of ideas. This is odd because reasoning about the public good is not something we simply consume. Reasoning

"The Art of Protesting During Donald Trump's Presidency," by Jeremy David Bendik-Keymer, The Conversation, January 20, 2017. https://theconversation.com/the-art-of-protesting-during-donald-trumps-presidency-71460. Licensed under CC BY-ND 4.0 International.

doesn't work like that. You have to ask what makes sense, not whether you simply want it.

Brown also discusses how students and families often value education by its "return on investment." This displaces deeper values such as growing up or becoming a good human being and an active citizen. Learning to govern our lives through shared rule is replaced by outperforming other competitive individuals.

In examples such as these, Brown shows how our capacity to work together is undermined in the way that we think. From the macro level of constitutional interpretation to the micro level of getting an education, neoliberalism "hollows out" our ability to think collectively about things.

Saying "We" and Meaning It

Thankfully, the ideas in the concept of protest can address this threat.

"Protest" has a Latin root that means to bear witness publicly. The idea is that in protest, some of us step forth and share something we think should be considered by all.

"Democracy" has a Greek root that means that the people have the power to construct society. We interpret this in the United States as rule by and for the people. The idea is that power is shared between us.

Now there can be no sharing when we can't say "we" and mean it. Someone is being left out.

Furthermore, the minute we can say "we" and mean it, we affirm our shared volition. When we can attach our wills to something and affirm it, we share (some) power.

Thus, sharing power between people demands that people can say "we" sincerely and without reservation, and that they have not succumbed to oppression in the moment of speaking.

Democratic protest is at heart, I think, the act of finding how we can arrive at a point to say "we" and mean it. "How can we?!" we say in protest. But we also say, "How can we?" (notice the punctuation). "We the people" isn't just an assumption of democracy, it is democracy's goal and ideal.

Clearing a Space for Each Other

If the main threat to democracy today is the loss of collective thinking, then protest is democracy's guardian. But protesters must develop the idea of sharing power. Where can we turn to do this?

Today, some of the most exciting work on sharing is found in what is called "socially engaged art." Artists such as Chloë Bass, Caroline Woolard and Michael Rakowitz have created ways of sharing power and of protesting that reinvigorate community and democracy.

Rakowitz urged that the color orange be removed from the city of Cleveland to protest the killing of Tamir Rice after he'd removed the orange safety tip from his toy gun.

Woolard has formed barter schools for knowledge in a "solidarity economy" where knowledge can be shared even when you cannot afford university.

Bass has given people the opportunity to better understand what living with others means through a series of interactive exercises. She gets at underlying fears through rituals people can trust.

These aesthetic acts are aimed at bringing people together across boundaries so that we are able to say "we." They provide opportunities to work through trauma, impotence or class inequality and exclusion. They open up communication.

Protesters can learn from socially engaged art. Why shout at the police when they aren't listening? It's more imaginative to organize different ways to hear each other.

Corporations Have Tremendous Global Influence

Ryan Cristián

Ryan Cristián is the founder and editor in chief of the Last American Vagabond.

It is quite incredible that the unelected bureaucrats of the EU Commission are even entertaining such an idea as the deeply unpopular TTIP trade deal amid huge citizen protest whilst already facing multiple episodes of social, political and economic unrest and crisis as the demise of the European project gathers pace.

The EU is experiencing extensive political threats and upheaval from left and right of centre political groups angry at EU imposed austerity. Greece is being raped by its so-called partners and it is just one of several other EU states en-route to ruin.

The declining global economic picture provides all the more reason for the corporations to look for new avenues of revenue. But which businesses are pushing most for the proposed EU-US trade deal TTIP? And who is really influencing EU negotiators? And just how are the rights of European citizens represented in the biggest trade deal in history?

Just in Brussels alone, there are now over 30,000 corporate lobbyists, shadowy agitators as The Guardian puts it, who are responsible for influencing three-quarters of legislation in the EU. But even they are left in the shade when it comes to the power being afforded to corporations in the TTIP negotiations.

The US Chamber of Commerce, the wealthiest of all US corporate lobbies, and DigitalEurope (whose members include all the big IT names, like Apple, Blackberry, IBM, and Microsoft) are there.

"Meet the Corporations Lobbying Hardest for Ttip and the End of Democracy," by Ryan Cristián , The Last American Vagabond, February 19, 2016. https://www.thelastamericanvagabond.com/business/meet-corporations-lobbying-hardest-ttip-end-democracy/ Licensed under CC BY-ND 4.0 International.

BusinessEurope, the European employers' federation and one of the most powerful lobby groups in the EU are there.

Transatlantic Business Council, a corporate lobby group representing over 70 EU and US-based multinationals. ACEA, the car lobby (working for BMW, Ford, Renault, and others) and CEFIC, the Chemical Industry Council (lobbying for BASF, Bayer, Dow, and the like) are all there.

European Services Forum, a lobby outfit banding together large services companies and federations such as Deutsche Bank, Telefónica, and TheCityUK, representing the UK's banking industry are there as are Europe's largest pharmaceutical industry association (representing some of the biggest and most powerful pharma companies in the world such as GlaxoSmithKline, Pfizer, Eli Lilly, Astra Zeneca, Novartis, Sanofi, and Roche).

FoodDrinkEurope, the biggest food industry lobby group (representing multinationals like Nestlé, Coca Cola, and Unilever) are sitting at the negotiating table as well.

However, 20% of all corporates lobbying the EU trade department are not listed on the EU's transparency register. This amounts to 80 organisations. Industry associations such as the world's largest biotechnology lobby BIO, US pharmaceutical lobby group PhrMA, and the American Chemical Council are lobbying in the shadows. More than one-third of all US companies and industry associations which have lobbied on TTIP (37 out of 91) are not in the EU register. Even Levi Jeans lurks in this murky group unwilling to publicly identify themselves.

The EU Commission even decided in its wisdom that its "transparency" register was not mandatory or the issues being lobbied on do not require admission in any way. Hardly transparent.

The United States has achieved most of the privately held meetings behind closed doors. They represent the top ten of biggest spenders of all lobbyists. ExxonMobil, Microsoft, Dow, Google, and General Electric all spend more than €3 million per year on lobbying the EU institutions.

Big pharmaceutical organisations have stepped up their lobbying for TTIP and this is particularly worrying. The pharmaceutical sector is pushing for a TTIP agenda with potentially severe implications for access to medicines and public health. Longer monopolies through strengthened intellectual property rules and limits on price-controlling policies in TTIP could drive up prices for medicines and costs for national health systems. Misery and death in exchange for profit.

The banking sector have lobbied hard for financial regulations that they would like to see scrapped via TTIP. From US rules on capital reserves (which require companies to keep aside a proportion of capital available to avoid risk of collapse or bailout), to regulations on too-big-to-fail foreign banks. Big finance on both sides of the Atlantic is also lobbying for a dedicated TTIP chapter on financial regulation, which could lead to the delay, watering down, or outright block of much-needed reform and control of the financial sector necessary to avoid another financial meltdown. Where is the sense in that?

When European Trade Commissioner Cecilia Malmström took office in November 2014 she promised a "fresh start" for the TTIP negotiations, including more civil society involvement and listening to public concerns as her "top priority." Lets not forget that the EU Commission undertook the largest ever survey of the EU bloc on the subject in 2014 and garnered 150,000 responses, more than 100 times more than any previous consultation on trade—and admitted that the majority of respondents expressed fears that the deal's investment clauses would undermine national sovereignty. What the Commission did not say was of that 150,000, 97% were opposed to TTIP.

In the first six months since Malmström took office, she, her Cabinet and the director general of the EU trade department had 121 one-on-one lobby meetings behind closed doors in which TTIP was discussed. No less than 83% of these declared meetings were with business lobbyists—but only 16.7% were held with public interest groups.

The fact that Malmström and her team seem to primarily deal with the arguments of business representatives raises serious concerns that industry lobbyists continue to dominate the agenda of the TTIP talks and crowd out citizens' interests. It is noteworthy that in a meeting with French employer's federation (MEDEF) on 26 March 2015, for example, the EU trade department was warned that "the 19 million European SMEs which do not export will face increased competition" from TTIP.

To fully gauge who is being listened to one only has to read that of 597 closed-door TTIP meetings in the period 2102-14, only 53 or 9% were represented by public interest groups. And nothing has improved.

A small example of corporations over people, came about in 2012 when the trade department within the EU specifically contacted the crop pesticides industry who were actively encouraged to "identify opportunities of closer cooperation." The response was that CropLife America demanded "significant harmonisation" for pesticide residues in food. Trade unions, environmentalists, and consumer groups did not receive such special invites.

Likewise, The Association of Automotive Suppliers (CLEPA), got an email from the EU Trade department thanking "you for your readiness to work with us," and offering a meeting, "to discuss about your proposal, ask for clarification and consider next steps." Again, public interest groups did not receive this special treatment.

Another example of the formidable alliance between EU negotiators and the corporate sector are the two most powerful lobby groups invited to "co-write" TTIP regulations by the EU trade department. Another is the enthusiasm in the financial lobby community for the EU's approach on financial regulation in TTIP. When the EU's position on the issue was leaked in early 2014, Richard Normington, Senior Manager of the Policy and Public Affairs team at TheCityUK—a key British financial lobby group —applauded the Commission's proposals, because it "reflected so closely the approach of TheCityUK that a bystander would have thought it came straight out of our brochure on TTIP."

The largest single petition in history was against Monsanto with a staggering 2.1 million signatures that has since been eclipsed by the petition StopTTIP that has garnered 3.3 million signatures. But this single petition is massively overshadowed by the millions involved in protests groups all over Europe. The goal is to arrest the corporate coups d'état of Europe currently being facilitated by people like David Cameron, Cecilia Malmström and Barack Obama.

For Britain, in the firing line of that take-over by corporations is the NHS, food and environmental safety, regulations to stop an out-of-control banking industry, privacy, security and jobs to name just a few. Most importantly, our hard-fought for democracy is not just undermined—it's for sale to the highest bidder.

Conservative Lawmakers Strive to Limit Protesters' Rights

Laura Graham

Laura Graham is assistant professor of sociology at Trinity College Dublin. Her current research focuses on Black Lives Matter and policing and justice in Ferguson, Missouri. She also writes about the Trump administration and US politics.

Civil protest is a crucial tenet of any free democracy—and in the US it's protected by the Constitution's first amendment. But a wave of new anti-protest laws may infringe on this hard-won constitutional right—one that could scarcely be more deeply rooted in the American political psyche.

On December 16, 1773, a band of protesters boarded the East India Company's ship in Boston and, in defiance of the Tea Act tax, tossed the entire shipment of tea into the harbour. Now known as the Boston Tea Party, this illegal act of civil disobedience helped spark the American Revolution. It remains one of the US's core patriotic narratives, the embodiment of the idea that freedom of protest and dissent is a central principle of democracy.

This right has been enshrined in American democratic dogma since the Bill of Rights was introduced in the Constitution in 1789. In fact, the Founding Fathers believed the right to protest was so important that they addressed it in the first amendment to the Constitution:

> Congress shall make no law respecting an establishment of religion, or prohibiting the free exercise thereof; or abridging the freedom of speech, or of the press; or the right of the people peaceably to assemble, and to petition the government for a redress of grievances.

"New Protest Laws Are Incompatible with American Democracy," by Laura Graham, The Conversation, April 7, 2017. https://theconversation.com/new-anti-protest-laws-are-incompatible-with-american-democracy-74279. Licensed under CC BY-ND 4.0 International.

The right is reinforced by the 14th amendment, which prohibits states from violating the first amendment. Despite this important constitutional protection, lawmakers across the states have introduced legislation that threatens to infringe on citizens' first amendment rights.

Clamping Down

Several states have seen legislation passed or bills proposed that would seriously curtail protest activity. In North Dakota and Tennessee, bills have been put forward that would make it legal for motorists to run over and kill protesters so long as it isn't their specific intent. In Iowa, a bill proposes that protesters stopping traffic will be charged with a felony that carries up to five years in prison and a $7,500 fine. Indiana lawmakers have proposed a bill that would allow police to use any force necessary to remove protesters from blocking traffic.

Minnesota legislators put forward a law that would allow the state to sue convicted protesters for the cost of policing and providing security at demonstrations. In Washington state, a bill would label protests as "economic terrorism."

Virginia legislators are also considering a bill that would increase the penalties for failing to disperse from a protest, fining protesters up to $2,500 and serving as much as a year in jail. And, in North Carolina, a lawmaker has proposed a bill making it a criminal offence for a protester to "threaten, intimidate, or retaliate against a present or former North Carolina official in the course of, or on account of, the performance of his or her duties."

Federally, the Trump administration is abundantly clear about where it stands on anti-government protest. The new whitehouse. gov website features a page headed: "Standing Up For Our Law Enforcement Community," which puts it bluntly: "Our job is not to make life more comfortable for the rioter, the looter, or the violent disrupter."

See You in Court

In an age of political turmoil, highlighted by the election of a presidential candidate who lost the popular vote by nearly 3m, the right to protest is surely as critical as ever—and yet it is facing serious challenges.

True, it is not in itself unconstitutional for state or federal government to impose restrictions on protest activity, including requiring permits for peaceable assembly and prohibiting protesters from blocking traffic and other threats to public safety. Similarly, while many forms of protest are protected on public property, civil disobedience on private property is not a protected right. Indeed, restrictions on protest have existed for quite some time.

What's changing are the penalties for violating protest restrictions, which are in many cases far greater than they have been in the past. The question, then, is whether these laws and the penalties they impose will actually work.

After all, when direct action is used to protest something, breaking the law is often part of the point. New legislative crackdowns are unlikely to deter movements such a #BlackLivesMatter and #NoDAPL, whose members are very much aware that even Gandhi broke laws to protest injustice—a concept known as *satyagraha* or "truth force" in Gandhian non-violence philosophy.

So do the laws now advancing through state legislatures really pose an existential threat to American democracy? Many protesters and Trump opponents might think so—but on balance, if protesters end up taking their cases to court, their first amendment rights will probably be upheld. While some of the new laws may be found constitutional in protection of public safety—as the saying goes: "your rights end where mine begin"—others stand a good chance of being struck down for violating protesters' rights to freedom of peaceable assembly.

So while the conservative lawmakers advancing these bills may be able to get them through state houses—and while the White House may apparently share their desire to curb protesters' freedoms —they might yet be denied their wishes by the Constitution's most basic principles.

Organizations to Contact

The editors have compiled the following list of organizations concerned with the issues debated in this book. The descriptions are derived from materials provided by the organizations. All have publications or information available for interested readers. This list was compiled on the date of publication of the present volume; the information provided here may change. Be aware that many organizations take several weeks or longer to respond to inquiries, so allow as much time as possible.

Better Business Bureau (BBB)
Council of Better Business Bureaus
3033 Wilson Blvd, Suite 600
Arlington, VA 22201
703-276-0100
website: http://www.bbb.org

The Better Business Bureau's mission is to be a leader in advancing marketplace trust by doing the following: setting standards for marketplace trust; encouraging and supporting best practices by engaging with and educating consumers and businesses; celebrating marketplace role models; calling out and addressing substandard marketplace behavior; and creating a community of trustworthy businesses and charities.

Democratic National Committee
430 South Capitol Street Southeast
Washington, DC 20003
202-863-8000
website: http://www.democrats.org

The current platform set forth by the Democratic National Committee represents the ideas and beliefs that govern the Democratic Party. This includes raising incomes and restoring economic security for the middle class, creating good-paying jobs, fighting for economic fairness and against inequality, and several related goals with the same objective in mind. The organization's preamble includes the following statement: "Democrats believe that cooperation is better than conflict, unity is better than division, empowerment is better than resentment, and bridges are better than walls."

Federal Trade Commission
600 Pennsylvania Avenue NW
Washington, DC 20580
202-326-2222
website: http://www.ftc.gov

The FTC's mission is to prevent business practices that are anticompetitive or deceptive or unfair to consumers; to enhance informed consumer choice and public understanding of the competitive process; and to accomplish this without unduly burdening legitimate business activity. Its goals include protecting consumers, maintaining competition, and advancing performance.

National Association for the Advancement of Colored People (NAACP)
4805 Mt. Hope Drive
Baltimore, MD 21215
877-NAACP-98
website: http://www.naacp.org

The National Association for the Advancement of Colored People's mission is to to ensure the political, educational, social, and economic equality of rights of all persons and to eliminate race-based discrimination. The organization was founded in 1909 and has more than a half-million members. Its vision is to ensure a society in which all individuals have equal rights without discrimination based on race.

National Institute for Lobbying and Ethics (NILE)
703-383-1330
website: http://www.lobbyinginstitute.com

The National Institute for Lobbying and Ethics was founded in 2016 in response to the shutdown of the Association of Government Relations Professionals. NILE's Code of Ethics includes the following articles: honesty and integrity; compliance with applicable laws, regulations, and rules; professionalism;conflicts of interest; due diligence and best efforts; compensation and engagement terms; confidentiality; public education; and duty to governmental institutions.

National Organization for Women (NOW)
1100 H Street NW, Suite 300
Washington, DC 20005
202-628-8669
website: http://www.now.org

Founded in 1966, NOW works in all fifty states to promote feminist ideals, lead societal change, eliminate discrimination, and achieve and protect the equal rights of all women and girls in all aspects of social, political, and economic life. The organization focuses on six core issues: reproductive rights and justice, economic justice, ending violence against women, racial justice, LGBTQ rights, and constitutional equality.

Republican National Committee
310 First Street SE Washington, DC 20003
202-863-8500
website: http://www.gop.com

The current platform set forth by the Republican National Committee represents the ideas and beliefs that govern the Republican Party. This includes restoring the American Dream; a rebirth of constitutional government; agriculture, energy, and the environment; government reform; great American families, education, healthcare, and criminal justice; and related goals with the same objective in mind.

Transatlantic Business Council (TABC)

919 18th Street NW, Suite 220
Washington, DC 20006
202-828-9104
website: http://www.transatlanticbusiness.org

The Transatlantic Business Council represents businesses headquartered in the EU and United States and defines itself as the main business interlocutor to both the US government and the EU institutions on issues impacting the transatlantic economy.

United States Office of Government Ethics (OGE)

1201 New York Avenue NW, Suite 500
Washington, DC 20005
202-482-9300
website: http://www.oge.gov

The US Office of Government Ethics's mission is to provide overall leadership and oversight of the executive branch's ethics program designed to prevent and resolve conflicts of interest. The vision of this office is to achieve a high level of public confidence in the integrity of executive branch programs and operations.

US Chamber of Commerce

1615 H Street NW
Washington, DC 20062-2000
202-659-6000
website: http://www.uschamber.com

The US Chamber of Commerce represents the interests of more than three million businesses of all sizes, sectors, and regions. It was founded in 1912, under President Taft.

Bibliography

Books

Louise Chappell and Lisa Hill (editors). *The Politics of Women's Interests: New Comparative Perspectives*. New York, NY: Taylor & Francis, 2016.

Thomas R. Dye. *Who's Running America?* New York, NY: Routledge, 2014.

Martin Gilens. *Affluence and Influence: Economic Inequality and Political Power in America*. New York, NY: Princeton University Press and the Russell Sage Foundation, 2012.

Matt Grossman. *New Directions in Interest Group Politics*. New York, NY: Routledge 2013.

Matt Grossman. *The Not-So-Special Interests*. Stanford, CA: Stanford University Press, 2012.

Jacob Hacker and Paul Pierson. *Winner-Take-All-Politics: How Washington Made the Rich Richer—and Turned Its Back on the Middle Class*. New York, NY: Simon and Schuster, 2010.

Thomas T. Holyoke. *Interest Groups and Lobbying: Pursuing Political Interests in America*. University of California, Fresno, CA: Westview Press, 2014.

Ronald J. Hrebenar. *Interest Group Politics in the Southern States*. University of Alabama Press: 2015.

William P. Kreml. *Losing Balance: The De-Democratization of America*. New York, NY: Taylor & Francis, 2016

James Strock. *Disruptpolitics.us*. Serve to Lead Group, 2016.

Benjamin C. Waterhouse. *Lobbying America: The Politics of Business from Nixon to NAFTA*. Princeton, NJ: Princeton University Press, 2014.

Periodicals and Internet Sources

Max Cherney, "The Politics of Pot: the Marijuana Industry is Now a Special Interest Group," Vice News, October 4, 2015. news.vice.com/article/the-politics-of-pot-the-marijuana-industry-is-now-a-special-interest-group.

G. William Domhof, "The Class-Domination Theory of Power," University of California at Santa Cruz, updated February 2012. www2.ucsc.edu/whorulesamerica/power/class_domination.html.

Jeffrey Folks, "The Growing Tyranny of the Political Elite," American Thinker, February 27, 2013. www.americanthinker.com/articles/2013/02/the_growing_tyranny_of_the_political_elite.html.

Martin Gilens and Benjamin I. Page, [abstract] "Testing Theories of American Politics: Elites, Interest Groups, and Citizens," Cambridge Core, Cambridge University Press, September 18, 2014.

Catherine Ho, "Interest Groups Trying to Get Pet Projects into State of Union May Be Disappointed," *Washington Post*, January 11, 2016.

Nicholas Leman, "Conflict of Interests," *New Yorker*, August 11, 2008. www.newyorker.com/magazine/2008/08/11/conflict-of-interests.

Alain Sherter, "When it Comes to Lobbying, One Group Stands Out," CBS News, August 4, 2015. www.cbsnews.com/news/when-it-comes-to-lobbying-one-group-stands-out.

"Texas Politics: Lobbying," University of Texas at Austin, 2006. www.laits.utexas.edu/txp_media/html/ig/0601.html.

Paul D. Thacker and Curt Furberg, "In Science, Follow the Money, if You Can," *LA Times*, May 12, 2016. www.latimes.com/opinion/op-ed/la-oe-0512-thacker-furberg-transparency-science-20160512-story.html.

Index

A

AARP, 24, 28, 29, 30, 79, 109
Adelson, Sheldon, 23
"Advancing the Empirical
    Research on Lobbying,"
    109
Affordable Care Act, 24, 25
AFL-CIO, 22, 28, 62, 71
Alexander, Rachel, 102–105
American Bar Association, 68
*American Democracy in an Age
    of Rising Inequality*, 87
American Federation of State,
    County, and Municipal
    Employees (AFSCME),
    28, 102, 103, 104
American Israel Public Affairs
    Committee (AIPAC), 23
American Medical
    Association (AMA),
    24–25, 62, 68
Americans for Prosperity,
    23–24
Amy, Douglas J., 84–101
anti-change interest groups,
    34–35
Arjun, K., 42–45
Australia, lobbying in, 36–40

B

Bendik-Keymer, Jeremy,
    115–117
Berry, Jeffrey, 69
biased pluralism, 77, 78, 108,
    109
Bork, Robert, 22
Bourdieu, Pierre, 47–48
Brown, Wendy, 115, 116
Bush, George H.W., 64
Bush, George W., 27, 64, 97, 102
Bush, Jeb, 51
businesses, how they work as
    interest groups, 67

C

campaign financing, and
    contributions from the
    political left, 102–105
Citizens United v. FEC, 104,
    115
Clinton, Bill, 27, 64, 74
Clinton, Hillary, 51, 52, 53, 64
Corley, Danielle, 13, 27–31
corporations, and global
    political influence, 14,
    90–94, 118–122
Cristián, Ryan, 14, 118–122

D

Dakota Access Pipeline, 112
Distinctions, 47

E

Earl, Jennifer, 14, 111–114
economic elite domination, 77,
    78, 79, 80, 82, 108, 109
elite theory
    compared to interest group
        theory, 63–64
    compared to oligarchy and
        aristocracy, 42–45
    and control of society's
        resources, 46–50
    elites as class, 48–50, 51–54

F

"Federalist No.10," 30, 62
Figueiredo, John M. de, 109
flash activism, 112, 113–114
Foucault, Michel, 115
free rider problem, 69, 71, 72

G

Gilens, Martin, 27–31, 77–83,
    107–109
Graham, Laura, 14, 123–125
Green Garage, 17–20

H

Hacker, Jacob, 90, 109
Hays, R. Allen, 65–76
Heritage Foundation, 23, 70
hyperpluralism, 20

I

informative lobbying, 32, 33,
    73–74, 94–95
interest group theory, 62–64
intergovernmental groups,
    as special interest group,
    68–69
International Brotherhood of
    Teamsters, 28

K

Kelleher, Brian, 109
"Kony 2012," 113

L

Leach, Michelle, 13, 21–26
Letts, Quentin, 59
"liberal metropolitan elite,"
    criticism of term, 14,
    55–57, 58–60
lobbying, methods of, 33–35,
    36–40

M

Madison, James, 30, 62, 63
Madland, David, 13, 27–31
majoritarian electoral
    democracy, 77, 78, 80, 108
majoritarian pluralism, 77, 78,
    108
Maximino, Martin, 107–110
*McCutcheon v. Federal Election
    Commission*, 83
Medicaid, 25, 98
Medicare, 12, 21, 24, 25, 99
Mills, C. Wright, 63, 77
Moveon.org, 23, 92, 114

N

Nader, Ralph, 62, 69
National Abortion and
    Reproductive Rights
    Action League, 22
National Association for the
    Advancement of Colored
    People (NAACP), 18, 21,
    22, 62, 66
National Conference of State
    Legislatures, 69
National Education
    Association, 28, 104
National Governors Association
    (NGA), 28, 29, 30, 69
National Labor Relations Act, 67
National Organization for
    Women (NOW), 18

National Rifle Association, 19,
    25–26, 62, 72, 79, 104
National Right to Life
    Committee, 22
neoliberalism, explanation of,
    115
Newtown shooting, 25
nongovernmental
    organizations (NGOs), 70

O

Obama, Barack, 21, 23, 25, 98,
    100, 113
Occupy Wall Street, 23, 52
oligarchy, 43, 81
Olson, Mancur, 71
*One Nation Uninsured: Why
    the U.S. Has No National
    Health Insurance*, 99
online activism, 111–114
online petitions, 111

P

Page, Benjamin, 77–83,
    107–109
Pierson, Paul, 90, 109
political activism/protest, 14,
    52, 111–114, 115–117,
    123–125
populism, Donald Trump and,
    51–54
pro-change interest groups,
    33–34

professional associations, as special interest group, 68
Public Citizen, 69
public interest groups, as special interest group, 69–70

Q

Qaudagno, Jill, 99

R

Rennie, George, 36–40
Rundell, Michael, 14, 58–60

S

Sanders, Bernie, 51
Schmidt, Natalie, 13, 51–54
Shorthouse, Ryan, 14, 55–57
Sierra Club, 22, 70
Soros, George, 23
special interest groups
  benefits of, 18–19
  history of, 67–70
  how they lobby, 32–35, 36–40, 93–94
  liabilities of, 19–20, 70–76
  pervasiveness of government influence, 32, 65–67, 84–100
"stop-and-frisk" policy, 21
Supreme Court justice nominations, 22
Swift, James, 77–83

T

"Testing Theories of American Politics: Elites, Interest Groups and Average Citizens," 77–83, 107–109
Tocqueville, Alexis de, 62, 77
Toledo, University of, 62–64
Trump, Donald, 51–54, 111, 115, 124

U

unions, as representatives of middle class, 13, 27–31, 67–68
United Auto Workers, 28, 79
universities, as special interest group, 28, 29, 30
U.S. Chamber of Commerce, 24, 25, 29, 67, 103, 118

V

Vergara, Luis Garrido, 13, 46–50

W

Weber, Max, 47, 49
Winner-Take-All Politics: Public Policy, Political Organization and the Precipitous Rise of Top Incomes in the United States, 90, 109
Wolton, Stephane, 13, 32–35